Red Chips

and the globalisation of China's enterprises

Red Chips

and the globalisation of China's enterprises

Charles de Trenck

Simon Cartledge

Anil Daswani

Christian A Katz

David Sakmar

Asia 2000 Limited
Hong Kong

ISBN 962-7160-64-4

Published by Asia 2000 Ltd
1101 Seabird House,
22–28 Wyndham Street, Central,
Hong Kong

http://www.asia2000.com.hk/

Typeset with Ventura Publisher in Palatino by Asia 2000
Printed in Hong Kong by Regal Printing

First edition 1997
Second revised edition 1998

Distributed in the United States by
University of Washington Press
PO Box 50096, Seattle, WA 98145

and in Canada by
University of British Columbia Press
6344 Memorial Road, Vancouver, BC V6T 1Z2

The opinions, comments and recommendations expressed in this book are entirely those of the authors and do not necessarily represent the views of their employers.

[The model king] graduates the taxes, rectifies the affairs of government, and develops the myriad things, thereby nourishing the myriads of people. From the production of the fields, the tax rate is one part in ten. At border stations and in the markets, goods are inspected, but imposts are not levied. The use of mountains, forests, marshes and weirs is permitted or forbidden according to the season, but excises are not assessed. Land is inspected as to quality, and the rate of taxation set accordingly. The distance over which goods travel is taken into account in setting tribute payments. Those who are nearby will not hide their abilities and those who are distant will not hate their toilsome tasks. There will be no part of the country, however secluded or out of the way, where men will not hasten to serve and find peace and contentment in his rule.

Xunzi (circa 310–circa 213 BC)
"On the Regulations of a King", *Xunzi,* Book 9
(translated in Knoblock's *Xunzi,* 1990)

Socialists should insist on using the nationalised industries not simply to out-capitalise the capitalists — an attempt that may or may not succeed — but to evolve a more democratic and dignified system of industrial administration, a more humane employment of machinery, and a more intelligent utilisation of the fruits of human ingenuity and effort. If they can do that, they have the future in their hands. If they cannot, they have nothing to offer that is worthy of the sweat of free-born men.

E. F. Schumacher
Small is Beautiful, 1973

Contents

	PREFACE	13
	Chapter Overview	14
	ACKNOWLEDGMENTS	16
	NOTES ON CONTRIBUTORS	17
1	*CHINESE CAPITALISM AND CHINESE COMPANIES*	19
	Clarifying key terms	19
	Finding a point of departure	20
	State dinosaurs and unemployment	21
	Is merger mania around the corner?	23
	The planned economy: still ticking	24
	Major types of state-backed firms: A first look at H shares and red chips	25
	The fixation on property	26
	China's corporate role models	27
	Breaking down economic growth into stages	31
	Conclusion	34
	Appendix 1A: Chronology of events 1976–97	36
	Appendix 1B: A summary of China's economy in graphs	40
2	*THE GROWTH OF CHINA'S KEY CONGLOMERATES*	43
	Alphabet soup: What is a red chip?	43
	What does a red chip conglomerate do?	44
	What do H, B or N shares do?	45
	Reversal of fortune	45
	The road to establishing a conglomerate	46
	Understanding how funds are raised and invested	47

Behind the ratings game 48
Adding up the numbers 50
Is everything on the balance sheet? 50
Of misdirected investments and cheap funding 51
The difference between Hong Kong and mainland cost of capital 52
1997 and the cost of capital 53
Confusing the short and long term 54
How to build and operate a Chinese conglomerate
with a listed red chip 55
Property investments 57

Appendix 2A: Leading conglomerates 58
BEIJING ENTERPRISES 58
CHINA AEROSPACE 59
CHINA CEROIL FOOD 60
CHINA EVERBRIGHT 60
CHINA INTERNATIONAL TRUST AND INVESTMENT CORP 61
CHINA MERCHANTS 63
CHINA NATIONAL NON-FERROUS METALS 65
CHINA OCEAN SHIPPING CO 66
CHINA OVERSEAS HOLDINGS 67
CHINA RESOURCES (HOLDINGS) 67
CHINA TRAVEL SERVICE (HOLDINGS) HK LTD 69
GUANGDONG ENTERPRISES (HOLDINGS) LTD 70
GUANGDONG INTERNATIONAL TRUST AND INVESTMENT CORP 71
NORTH CHINA INDUSTRIES 74
SHANGHAI INDUSTRIAL INVESTMENT (HOLDINGS) 75
SHOUGANG STEEL 76
YUE XIU ENTERPRISES 77
Appendix 2B: Red Chips 79

3 *A QUICK LOOK AT THREE VERY DIFFERENT COMPANIES* 81
COSCO: The new kid on the block 81
SHOUGANG STEEL: A model state company rocked by controversy 84
CHINA RESOURCES: The good corporate citizen 87

4 *Financing Chinese Conglomerates — The Banking System* 91
The emergence of a Chinese banking system 93
The state-governed development of a two-tier banking system 93
The challenge of transition: attempts at decentralisation 98
The "commercialisation" of the Chinese banking system 103
Bank-industry linkages in China 107

Appendix 4A: Selected Chinese bank profiles 113
BANK OF CHINA 113
INDUSTRIAL AND COMMERCIAL BANK OF CHINA 114
STATE DEVELOPMENT BANK 115
BANK OF COMMUNICATIONS 116
HUA XIA BANK 117
Appendix 4B: Foreign Banks in China 118
Appendix 4C: Funding for Chinese corporates 119

5 *CITIC Beijing* 121
History 125
Confusion over investment strategy 131
Discussion and conclusion 134

6 *CITIC Pacific* 139
Aviation interests 140
Telecommunications 143
Trading & distribution 145
Property 146
Consumer credit 149
Acquisitions and China infrastructure point the way forward 150
Power generation and a new push into PRC infrastructure 151
Industrial manufacturing facilities 152
Conclusion: does the counter deserve a PRC premium? 152

7 *GUANGDONG ENTERPRISES AND GUANGDONG INVESTMENT* 153
The Guangdong economic miracle 155
Is a fall from grace around the corner? 156
Contrasts between the economies of Guangdong and China 157
Differences between the parent and the listed flagship 158
What happened to 1992's assets? 163
How to give analysts a migraine 164
Guangdong Investment's blind spot: the hotel and tours division 165
A brief look at the listed company's cash flow statement 166
A brief history of acquisitions from the parent 168
Guangnan holding structure 175
A closer look at GEHL subsidiaries 176
Discussion of GDI operations 178
Conclusion: what next for the group? 181

8 *CHALLENGES TO REFORMING CHINA'S STEEL INDUSTRY* 183
China's steel industry: historical development and origins 184
Characteristics of the Stalinist model in the steel industry 186
Relationship with the Ministry of Metallurgical Industry 186
Anatomy of a state-owned enterprise in the steel sector 188
Prospects for reform and the future of SOEs 191

Appendix 8A: Steel production 196
Appendix 8B: Steel manufacturers 197

EPILOGUE 199

RED CHIPS: A CALL FOR ACTION 203

FURTHER DATA 207

BIBLIOGRAPHY, SOURCES 213

Tables

Table 2.1: Partial list of Red Chips listed in Hong Kong 79
Table 4.1: Comparison of China's four major banks 104
Table 4.2: The local presence of foreign banks in China 118
Table 4.3: Aggregated use of selected financing channels in China 120
Table 5.1: CITIC's year-end assets 123
Table 5.2: CITIC's pre-tax profits 124
Table 5.3: CITIC'S assets as percent of total assets 132
Table 5.4: Breakdown of CITIC's industrial assets 132
Table 6.1: CITIC Pacific property development schedule 148
Table 7.1: GEHL major subsidiaries, investments & projects 160
Table 7.2: Guangdong Investment corporate history 169
Table 8.1: Largest Chinese steel-makers and comparative statistics 197
Table X.1: China's top 20 foreign-funded enterprises 207
Table X.2: China 's largest industrials & trading companies 208
Table X.3: Selected China funds 208
Table X.4: Hong Kong–listed H Shares as at May 1997 210
Table X.5: US N share listings as at May 1997 212

Figures

1.1: Foreign exchange reserves, debt, direct investment	*40*
1.2: Growth of GNP, inflation, industry, CPI	*40*
1.3: Growth of exports and imports	*41*
2.1: The injection machine	*55*
2.2: Generic model for government-related conglomerates	*56*
3.1: Politics and share price performance	*86*
4.1: Sources of outside funding for Chinese corporates	*119*
5.1: CITIC Group	*122*
7.1: Guangdong and China GDP growth	*157*
7.2: Guangdong and China export growth	*157*
7.3: Guangdong Enterprises group chart	*158*
7.4: GE & GI operating profit margins	*162*
7.5: GE & GI net profit margins	*162*
7.6: Guangdong Enterprises' cost of debt	*164*
7.7: Guangnan holding structure — after sale to public and GDI	*175*
7.8: Guangnan holding structure — after partial resale back to parent	*175*
8.1: Steel production in the Deng era (1975–95)	*196*
8.2: Increase in GDP and steel production 1985–95	*196*
X.1: US$-Rmb exchange rates	*207*
X.2: China's exports by region, 1995	*209*
X.3: China's imports by region, 1995	*209*

Preface

Following works such as S. Gordon Redding's *The Spirit of Chinese Capitalism* in 1990, research into the rise of a Chinese form of capitalism has attracted a small following. But published work has so far focused on Overseas Chinese and their East Asia business networks. Most of what has been studied is the endless drive for entrepreneurship among family-centred companies. Amazingly enough there is little published in the English language on either Hong Kong Chinese, Taiwanese or mainland Chinese companies. The few books that are out there focus on the mavericks, their history and the development of their business savvy.

One of the more recent commentaries on the interaction between corporations and society is the analysis of Francis Fukuyama in his most recent book, *Trust*. His major conclusion regarding China and Chinese is that because of the closely knit family culture characteristic of Chinese and Overseas Chinese, large Chinese corporations are prevented from emerging. In societies where Chinese businesses operate, it would seem that the most suitable structures open to them are nimble, small outfits suited to changing market trends and the manufacturing sector. The higher functions of a corporation, ones relying on networks of professionals organised within social networks that support more dynamic interaction, are best left to what Fukuyama calls "high trust" societies such as Germany, Japan and the US. "Low trust" societies such as Italy and China fare badly when organisations are not set up along family lines. Though perhaps cast in too much of a Manichean black and white perspective, the issue raised is challenging and calls for more discussion.

Our current focus is on Chinese companies in operation today and the issues they face in developing into more mature corporations. In China it is not family lines that determine the formation of corporate structures, as has been established for companies run by Overseas Chinese around East Asia. Rather, it is governmental organisations, whether national, provincial or local. These government-backed Chinese corporate structures often follow a trail that leads back to foreign equity markets, particularly Hong Kong's stock exchange.

During and after our writing of this book, company structures continued to change. Any one company analysis in this book is likely to be in need of an update. China's equity markets are young and unpredictability is proving its only constant. However, conclusions from our analysis remain very similar irrespective of recent changes. At the time this book went to press, in September 1997, reforms were accelerating at a greater pace than anticipated just prior to Deng's death in February 1997. However these are proving to be the same reforms put forth in 1992. What this means is that though some of the numbers and facts are moving too fast for stationary objects such as books, key players and issues remain much the same.

Chapter Overview

Chapter 1 sets the backdrop of our analysis. Before looking at China's emerging corporations, we have to define the bounds in which they operate. At issue are questions as to what are the building blocks of a Chinese company and to what extent do the profit motive and the efficiencies that arise therefrom exist in Chinese firms. A brief economic and political history of China since 1979 is also provided for perspective, with additional macroeconomic data on China provided in the appendix.

Chapter 2 provides an overview of many of the major Chinese firms. The chapter is broken down into two major sections. The first surveys the formation of Chinese companies and issues regarding their financial and organisational structures. The second provides backgrounds on major groups and their corporate activities.

Chapter 3 singles out some noteworthy examples among China's leading companies, namely the infamous Shougang, the newly risen COSCO, and one of the more conservative Chinese companies, China Resources.

Chapter 4 surveys the current banking system and its relationships to the ailing state-owned enterprises. First, the chapter looks at China's leading banks, their history and current reforms. Second, the author looks at how Chinese companies can raise funds from banks and the equity markets — and what their track record has been. Profiles of several leading banks are also provided, including a look at the Bank of China, ICBC, the State Development Bank, Bank of Communications, and Hua Xia Bank.

Chapters 5 and 6 look at the CITIC group from two different perspectives. First, we dig into CITIC's overall operations and provide a profile of CITIC Beijing. CITIC's development can be broken down into a number of phases, characterised by the styles of those who were at the company's helm. In chapter 5, the focus is brought to bear on the Hong Kong listed subsidiary, CITIC Pacific, and a description of its major divisions and operations.

Chapter 7 looks at the relationship between Guangdong Enterprises and its listed subsidiary, Guangdong Investment. The focus of the piece is the complexity of the relationship between the holding and its listed company. The analysis provides readers with an understanding of the benefits gained by the holding company when it engages in complex injections into a listed vehicle.

Chapter 8 deals with the historic role of the steel industry, the problems of separating the sector from state planning, and management issues.

CdT

Acknowledgments

This book is a collaboration among several analysts, writers and businessmen who have covered China's economy and its budding corporate sector. At our disposal are dozens of books, studies, annual reports and equity research pieces. We have also relied on personal experiences, interviews and un-published interviews in putting together various chapters.

Grateful acknowledgment is made to a number of analysts, financial journalists and investors who have contributed their views and feedback while these chapters were being written. Those contributing their input include Jamie O'Donnell, Henny Sender, Wai Wai Yang, Bruce Gilley, Andrew Kuet, Andy Mantel, Dali Yang, Jane Tam and a number of others. Thanks go to these commentators for helping to soften some of the rougher edges of this short book. The arguments and views expressed in this book represent those of the authors only.

We hope readers will understand that this is a new field in which the major road signs have yet to be erected. Comments and queries can be made to cdt@hkstar.com.

CdT

Notes on contributors

Charles de Trenck currently works as an analyst at Credit Suisse First Boston in Hong Kong. He covered China as an analyst and a China research head for another regional brokerage from 1993 to 1996. Charles also worked for a European bank's China desk as a credit analyst covering Chinese companies and their Hong Kong subsidiaries between 1992 and 1993. He holds an MA in East Asian Literature from UCLA (1993), a Master of International Management from the American Graduate School of International Management (1988) and a BSc in Chinese and Asian Studies from Georgetown University (1985). His articles have appeared in a number of publications, including *Business China*, the *South China Morning Post* and *Lloyd's List Maritime Asia.*

Simon Cartledge has been based in Hong Kong as Senior Editor for the Economist Intelligence Unit's *Business China* since 1993. Before joining EIU, Simon worked as an editor for a wire service as well as an editor for a number of Beijing-based publications. He holds an MA in Politics from Edinburgh University (1985).

Anil Daswani is a conglomerates analyst for a US brokerage and is based in Hong Kong. Anil has covered Hong Kong equities for a number of regional brokerages since 1992, first as an industrials analyst and later as a conglomerates analyst. He holds a BSc (Hons) from the University of Bradford (1991) in Computer Science.

Christian A Katz is head of Asia research at London Forfaiting Company, a major international finance company based in the UK. He previously worked as a derivative securities and convertible bonds salesman for SBC Warburg in Zurich, and in Hong Kong, where he focused on Chinese capital markets and credit risk research. Christian wrote his PhD on international banking and the Chinese financial system at the University of St Gall, Switzerland, from where he graduated in 1993.

David Sakmar is Vice President of Planning and Development for Steel Industries, Inc. and has been involved in the China steel trade since 1992. David holds a BA, Economics from UC Santa Barbara (1986) and a Master of Pacific International Affairs from UC San Diego's Graduate School of International Relations (1991).

CHAPTER 1

Chinese capitalism and Chinese companies

Charles de Trenck

Were we to get down to a nitty-gritty analysis of Chinese companies, we would first have to establish the pre-conditions for an environment in which companies or corporations function. This would require several volumes aimed at answering a principal question: Does capitalism exist in today's China? Strictly speaking the appropriate answer is no. Capitalism, as it is known in OECD (Organisation for Economic Cooperation and Development) countries and some newly industrialised countries in the 1990s, is a complex socio-economic phenomenon that will not take root in China for perhaps another decade. What exists in China's private sector today is vigorous entrepreneurial activity at the small business level, which in no small part is due to reforms initiated by Deng Xiaoping. The entrepreneurial spirit is certainly a key ingredient of capitalism in developed countries. But it is not a sufficient condition for capitalism to work its wonder.

The socio-economic restructuring that is taking place in China's companies is without a doubt within China's top state companies. But it has yet to develop toward any system known in developed economies in which business units cut, redeploy or add assets in order to maximise profits. In short, the two main ingredients making up capitalism are 1) the entrepreneurial spirit and 2) structured social networks operating within the confines of companies. Both exist in China. But they are not synchronised to operate together.

Clarifying key terms

Corporations are complex structures that require, among other things, a legal system guaranteeing ownership rights of property and the means of production, a reasonably effective education system (to form the social capital behind a quality product), and funding to renew and improve both the means of production and the social capital. Mature corporations such as the multinational corporations (MNCs) of today can only originate from developed economies that have undergone their version of the industrial revolution and the subsequent transition to a service economy.

Given the streamlining of corporations in OECD countries since the 1980s, it is apparent that these corporations have matured in a post-industrial environment that has forced them to adapt or perish. It is not good enough to accept static definitions for a phenomenon as rich and complex as capitalism. So what we mean by "capitalism" and "corporation" today are only the cousins of what capitalism and companies were during the industrial revolution.

When we look at our income tax returns, and realise how our tax money is being spent, most of us are also aware that the "capitalism" of today includes a portion of yesterday's "socialism". Whatever our political views may be, most of us would accept that capitalism today has incorporated a greater sense of responsibility toward a developed economy's social fabric. New problems, such as structural unemployment, created as a result are another issue.

Finding a point of departure

Since 1979 and the beginning of Deng's reforms, China has progressed far enough to permit certain necessary conditions such as the securing of property rights, as in land use rights for periods of 50 and 70 years, and the right to retain profits. This has led individuals to seize opportunities and start their own businesses, usually oriented towards the service industry. Initiative taken at the level of the individual is perhaps the most important factor driving economic growth. But the appearance of this phenomenon does not mean that "Chinese capitalism" has matured to the point that the concept as it is known in OECD economies is even remotely similar to "Chinese capitalism". It could be argued that China has not yet encountered capitalism as a force driving the economy, which, of course, relates back to the question of democracy's relationship to capitalism. This is also a key topic, but one that will not be pursued here.

For the rapidly developing private sector of the economy, what we have witnessed most clearly is the part of capitalism we know so well in Western economies as *entrepreneurism*. It is also in this pursuit that Chinese the world over have made their greatest contribution. Enterprising individuals typically run smaller operations with little organisational structure outside the family. For the purpose of this book, these companies, for the most part, do not exhibit the features we are looking for in tracking the formation of large, internationally-oriented companies in China. We have taken as our focus the larger state- and local government-backed companies as the more established sector to examine. It is a good place to begin, given that very few detailed studies have been made on Chinese companies to date.

Ironically, it is not the appearance of equity markets and individual shareholders that heralds the development of capitalism. All indications to date are that Chinese shareholders are most concerned about generous dividend policies (payout ratios often exceed 40–50%, underscoring the lack of understanding of re-investment of profits in developed equity markets) and government policies toward quotas for new company listings. Over the last few years, authorities several times have killed rallies with threats of new equity issues to drown out interest. When the public responded with share sell-offs in the wake of such announcements, the government has been known to eat its words and to pledge embargoes on new share issues. Predictably, such embargoes then triggered a return to the markets. Seldom have shareholders been called on to influence the direction of company policies.

Also ironically, so far it is the public sector, or more accurately the vanguard of the public sector with quasi-private sector companies under their control (incorporated in Hong Kong or other overseas locations) that currently operate the next-closest business units to Western-style corporations. Summaries of these companies and their activities will be found in following chapters.

State dinosaurs and unemployment

That it is too early for OECD-like capitalism to take root is all the more apparent given what now appears as a very long road to restructuring the majority of state enterprises, which, after dropping from about 80% of industrial output a decade ago, now still account for more than 40%. Enterprises controlled at the state level (as opposed to regional and local), represent the backbone of industry. To starve these firms of subsidies and force them to abide by the laws of the market place would likely produce an economic shock wave that would send unemployment soaring overnight.

In the mid-1990s, the government allowed the number of bankruptcies to rise significantly. It also moved to a system of allowing unprofitable enterprises to merge with successful ones. One plan heralded as a catalyst for change has been a pilot project to reform 100 state enterprises from a pool of about 100,000. However ambitious the government's plans may be, outside observers continue to call for caution when evaluating government claims. If consolidation of state enterprises were to be too rapid, China's urban unemployment rate would jump from the official 4.8mn in 1995 to over 20mn in a matter of months or even weeks. One estimate has put the number of idle workers still on the books as employed at 20mn. A few restructuring exercises would be enough to redefine such workers as unemployed.

A sensitivity analysis of China's unemployment to economic growth would be an extremely useful illustration. For instance, the *Economic Daily*, 13 June 1996, listed the problem of a drop in export growth in 1996. The sluggishness experienced in 1996, itself related to shortfalls in VAT rebates from the government to enterprises, with some US$2.4bn still owed from 1995. The paper estimated that a drop in export growth from 22.9% in 1995 to 5% in 1996 would shave up to 1.5% off economic growth and result in a loss of up to 2.5mn jobs. These figures outline the point that a drop in output as a result of closing down inefficient enterprises, and a subsequent extended drop in economic growth to low single digits, or even negative economic growth as in Russia during the mid-1990s, could easily increase the number of unemployed by a factor of four. The figure of 20mn unemployed is a commonly quoted estimate, but the truth is that no one really knows how many workers would be put out of work from the closing of inefficient enterprises.

In May 1997 the press reported that a number of regional and municipal governments were planning to downsize staff in the state sector. The Shanghai Labour Bureau in May detailed plans to seek re-employment for up to 600,000 workers made redundant during the period 1996–99. Even Guangzhou, along with Shenzhen considered the migration magnet of China, has seen a drop-off in the number of immigrants as well as a rise in unemployment. The Guangzhou Statistics Bureau in May 1997 reported that it had recorded that over 50,000 workers had been made jobless during the first quarter of 1997. Seventy percent of the layoffs were in the state sector.

The catch-phrase of the late 1990s in China is *xia gang*, or a form of redundancy without going down officially on the books as unemployed. One recent way of poking fun at the long-term trends and the role China's leaders have played in setting these trends is a saying relating three forms of *xia*, or going down or descending. The first form of descending was initiated by Chairman Mao who, during the Cultural Revolution, asked intellectuals and others to descend to the countryside, *xia xiang* or *xia fang*, in order to learn more about the revolution. The second type was initiated by Deng Xiaoping and was known as *xia hai*, or going into business. The third form, *xia gang*, is attributed to Jiang Zemin and refers to the wave of layoffs just beginning to sweep the state sector.

Consider another way of looking at the threat of a jump in unemployment. The fastest growing part of the economy over the last 10 years has been rural enterprises. Firms operating at this level are known as township and village enterprises, or TVEs. Between 1984 and 1994, employment by TVEs grew from 52mn to 130mn and compares to employment of about 75mn at state-owned enterprises. To break the iron rice bowl at state and other laggard enterprises in earnest would, in all likelihood, require the forced redundancy of a sizable portion of all the jobs created at TVEs over the last decade.

Is merger mania around the corner?

One trend initiated in early 1996 is the merger of a number of listed firms. In February, three Shanghai B share companies producing stationery products, Wing Sung Stationery, Shanghai Hero, China First Pencil and Shanghai Fenghua Ball Pen (A shares for PRC nationals only), announced they were seeking to merge their operations. Until 1992, all four companies were under the control of the Shanghai Light Industry Bureau, so the announced merger did not lack a touch of irony. Another planned merger announced in February involved the consolidation of two bicycle manufacturers with B share listings, Shanghai Forever and Shanghai Phoenix. Perhaps one of the most substantial mergers is that of Yizheng Chemical's acquisition of loss-making Foshan Chemical in 1995. The acquisition led Yizheng to raise new funds from overseas investors and to issue new H shares following its original IPO in 1994. Mergers, however, are likely to take the slow lane over the next few years, as efficient mergers would lead to unbearable levels of unemployment. Ultimately though, mergers will prove to be the key element in reducing over-capacity.

The planned economy: still ticking

Consider the traditional way of allocating capital to most enterprises in China prior to the reforms of the 1980s. State firms would receive injections of capital at the beginning of the year, proceed with working capital needs (salaries for workers producing low-quality products with only marginal demand), and return surplus funds to the state at the end of the year. For the most part, this system is dying. However, the release of funds to behemoth state enterprises is still the standard in heavy industry, and is correlated to policies set out in the five-year plans, with the Ninth Five-Year Plan having begun in January 1996. In brief, bits and pieces of the Planned Economy are alive and well in today's China, despite talk of allowing state firms to go bankrupt. It is too early to withdraw state support for half of China's industrial capacity and the pace of reform in the sector will by necessity be slow.

To maintain social stability, the most painless way out of the state enterprise quagmire is for private industry to take over more and more of total industrial production over the next decade. In this way, the portion of the economy subsidising the weak and the inefficient will be in a better position to carry the burden. Taking this slow approach to restructuring will without a doubt cause long-term headaches and weak links across China's industries, but will mitigate sharp corrections in industrial output and economic growth.

Major types of state-backed firms: A first look at H shares and red chips

At the same time as we watch the private sector gradually eclipse the state industrial sector, we witness state-backed companies of every sort trying to reconfigure themselves into corporate entities. As yet these former state and semi-state enterprises are not corporations in the true sense, for they often could not function as independent units were they severed from governmental support. However, many of their subsidiaries are more likely to act as independent entities, with different risk profiles, than to act in unison with head office.

Today's enterprises are, for the most part, new entities that go through the motions of the accounting concept of a "going concern". Take away state subsidies, protectionist tariff barriers, tax holidays, and other forms of preferential treatment, and few of these companies could stand on their own merit, as has often been pointed out with the newly-created Hong Kong H and New York N shares. We will discuss this issue in detail when we discuss state-backed companies, with special focus on red chips and their holding companies (see Chapter 2). But we should note the distinction between the two major types of Chinese companies first:

H and *N shares* (and Shanghai and Shenzhen *B shares*) are usually state-run factories that have been selected by the government and restructured to allow the most attractive parts of the plant to be sold to foreign investors. The first plants to really undergo such a transformation for listing were in 1992 and 1993. This restructuring requires painstaking negotiation between foreign investment banks and Chinese state and company officials. After restructuring, the new company is often merely a fraction of the original enterprise, which, as in the case of Shanghai Petrochemical's 1993 listing, is the difference between selected buildings, plant and equipment and a complete town (including hotels, schools, housing and a college).

State-backed companies typically represent the interests of China's leading ministries, the State Council, and provincial and municipal authorities. These companies control companies in related industries around the country, or in their sphere of influence. At the same time, they will have their own favourite investments, which will typically include substantial property-related holdings. Also common to these companies is that they have almost all sought a listing in Hong Kong over the last decade. Many of these listings have been obtained by buying inactive listed companies and then injecting assets. A drawback to this practice is that injections are often non-core assets such as properties, and when key industrials are injected it is often as associates rather than as subsidiaries. Stakes in associates are usually less attractive because they offer little control or transparency to shareholders. We will explore corporate developments for these companies in the following chapters.

The fixation on property

We will set aside the issue of the development of the property market in China in our current study, except as it pertains to companies covered. In China, as in Hong Kong, one of the main drivers of the economy is property. Most Chinese companies want to get in on a Hong Kong, Beijing, Shanghai or Guangzhou property project. This fixation on property ownership could be interpreted in light of China's traditional absence of property rights for individuals. Under dynastic rule, only the aristocracy held and managed land, and after 1949 all land-ownership, or rather, land-management, rights were assumed by the state. When land-use rights became a reality during the 1980s, property booms became key elements of economic growth, especially in China's coastal cities.

One of the first points long-term China investors seek to clarify is how likely are funds being raised to be invested into property? Of course, there is much sense in seeking out the committed property developers in China. But there is no sense giving money to an industrial company so that it can redevelop its factory into a commercial plaza, as some investors have discovered the hard way.

China's corporate role models

Cutting-edge companies in China number no more than a dozen. The rest are burdened with legacies of inefficiency, compounded by the ignorance of how to use the new organisational tools of the information age. The first step in bridging the divide separating China firms from the OECD-capitalist firm is the implementation of a diagnostic procedure aimed at understanding how subsidiaries, divisions and departments within the same company act with the same independence as separate companies. Socialist economic thought in China has failed, not because of implementation problems, but because of breakdowns in human organisation and the failure to harness human potential. The breakdown is similar to problems experienced in other socialist countries. Irrespective of whether socialist programmes can work in China or other countries, China can learn from countries and companies coming from similar backgrounds. Models developed in Taiwan, Singapore and France are all fair game for adaptation by Chinese companies in their search to develop their own version of the modern corporation.

1: Learning from China's smaller firms

Smaller entrepreneurial firms are for the most part excluded from the scope of this book. However, there are grounds for expecting some of these to take on the mantle of larger and more substantial companies within the next decade. A good place to look for these companies is in consumer-oriented businesses. To date, growth of consumer-driven operations in China has been dominated by Hong Kong companies such as Giordano, Goldlion, Chaifa and China-HK Photo. Some Chinese representatives in this group include Legend Holdings (Hong Kong listed), the Stone Group (Hong Kong listed) and Shanghai Dazhong Taxi (Shanghai listed). What these Chinese companies have in common is that they were formed within the last decade by individuals with few (or fewer) links to the state. Another commonality is their focus on the consumer side of the economy, though they too are often open to the standard gripe held by foreign investors regarding too much diversification. These companies can also suffer from a loss of direction as soon as a few key figures in management disappear.

2: Joint ventures can teach state companies a few more tricks

Taking a significant place within China's economy are MNCs and their joint ventures (JVs), which have typically come to China to manufacture labour-intensive products, and which, of course, take advantage of low wages relative to developed economies. MNCs have traditionally held the organisational talent and the investment capital; the Chinese JV partners, which nearly always represent government interests, have access to low-cost labour and the basic production facilities. MNCs have played a vital role in the development of China's technological capabilities and its export-oriented economy. Companies such as Motorola have added invaluable technological capabilities. Other companies such as Pilkington Glass have permitted Chinese companies to develop high-quality exports. In most cases, China could not have accessed new production technologies without these foreign firms. Foreign-funded enterprises accounted for 37% of China's total trade in 1994, or US$87.7bn out of US$236.7bn. The 1995 estimate rose to about 40%, and in 1996 to 43%.

Chinese firms face a number of organisational challenges before they can take on MNCs, even in China's own backyard. Consider a large MNC such as Dupont. It operates one of the first wholly foreign-owned enterprises in China and runs operations in Guangdong, Shanghai and Beijing, while at the same time accessing complementary operations around East Asia through a highly integrated organisational structure. Managers keep track of operational issues around China, and further afield, from their Beijing, Hong Kong, and other key Asian offices over a computer network. Production plants, offices, and personnel are managed from remote sites across Greater China. Chinese firms, at the moment, do not have the means to harness such economies of scale and multi-layered operational structures. With the exception of companies such as COSCO, they are barely in a position to connect their offices.

Beyond projects managed by the World Bank and consulting firms during the mid-1990s, the next logical step is for the formation of service-oriented JVs to undertake strategic re-organisation of China's major companies. Reorganisations would involve the formation of EDP, human resources, planning, R&D and other key departments along lines existing in developed countries. The relevance of this kind of restructuring cannot be over-emphasised.

3: Taiwan and Singapore companies offer new models
Chinese firms may only need to look to Taiwan to learn how to enhance their corporate structures. A number of companies have successfully grown, contrary to the argument put forth by Mr Fukuyama, beyond mere family companies to become sprawling conglomerates at the leading edge of innovation in East Asia. The thrust of Fukuyama's argument, that China, as a "low-trust" society, cannot grow beyond the family-dominated enterprise system heightens awareness of the issue of corporate governance in Chinese societies. He dismisses such a possibility, saying that "the *keiretsu* system, for example, would seem to be very difficult to export to a Chinese society." (*Foreign Affairs*, 1995, Volume 74 no. 5, p. 100). This dismissal points the direction to a new field of study. With groups such as CITIC already in existence for nearly 20 years, some Chinese conglomerates will invite comparisons with the likes of *keiretsu*s in Japan and with *chaebol*s in South Korea.

Existing models for China in Taiwan are already available, however. Companies such as Acer have grown into budding MNCs, and are able to take advantage of some of the same economies of scale as leading Western MNCs. Consider as well a company such as President Enterprises. The firm, which began in 1967 as a flour milling operation is today one of Taiwan's top ten enterprises, with operations spanning food processing, retailing and even securities trading. President has also expanded into the United States through acquisition. Moreover, President is one of the leading Taiwanese investors in China, with investments up to US$150mn, ranging from US$20mn for instant noodles in Kunshan, outside Shanghai, to US$10.5mn for tomato paste and juice in Xinjiang province.

Formosa Plastics is another example of a company that has grown enormously over the past decades and sought to develop investments in China. However, this time at least in partial agreement with Mr Fukuyama's thesis, a case might be made that the company has relied on a charismatic founder for its growth.

Mainland Chinese firms could also look to Singapore's model of what might be called state capitalism. In this city-state, government ministries have been credited with designing some of the world's best vocational training programmes as well as far-reaching investment strategies. Government-controlled groups such as the Keppel group of companies and Singapore Airlines are seen as very successful companies. These and many other companies are controlled by the government's investment arm, Temasek Holdings, while at the same time being listed on the Singapore stock exchange. In some circles, Singapore is seen as a strong contributor to China's attempts to improve its bureaucracy. The other main Singapore state company is the Government of Singapore Investment Corporation (GSIC), which shares many similar functions with Temasek. GSIC was established in 1981 with the mission of investing worldwide various funds at the disposal of the Singapore government.

4: Models of state-backed companies in France

Though difficult to compare on the same terms, France's socialist tradition of integrating the state and corporations also merits the attention of Chinese companies and the ministries that back them. To do this would require a survey of French government centralism (Paris as France's nerve centre), the examination of links between large state corporations and the state (such as Elf or Renault) and the operation of universities dedicated to the formation of business cadres (schools such as the Ecole Nationale d'Administration). France's state-controlled companies have been inching away from their socialist roots. Yet the system as it developed in post-WWII Europe remains a viable source of learning experiences for China's leadership.

5: Alternative Asian models

As mentioned above, South Korean conglomerates, or *chaebols*, invite comparisons with some of the high-profile Chinese companies. At least in theory. Researchers and some government officials have begun to consider the idea that Chinese leading companies should be encouraged to grow larger and take on the characteristics of *chaebols*, which include a high degree of centralisation of power combined with a broad degree of diversification among the operational divisions. In South Korea, *chaebol*s, though they have faced their own problems recently, have been credited with the rise to prominence of the automotive, steel, shipbuilding, electronics and other industries.

In that the *chaebol* represents a corporate structure that helped South Korea's economy to leapfrog to newly industrialised country (NIC) status using a hybrid of Korean, Western and Japanese corporate culture, some would propose that a similar model be used in China. One similarity that comes to mind is the strong ties between government and companies in both South Korea and China. One item that is absent in China thus far, however, has been the ability to mobilise large amounts of capital for investment in fixed assets capable of producing internationally competitive goods, particularly electronics, steel and automobiles.

Breaking down economic growth into stages

Since 1976 and the return of Deng Xiaoping to the political limelight, China has experienced a number of economic periods, each characterised by a different theme. Growth has been determined mostly by politics. The biggest engines of economic growth have been the export-oriented coastal regions and the special economic zones (SEZs) that dot these regions. The four periods together have been the story of restraining the country's unbounded drive for double-digit growth. China had very few macro-economic tools at its disposal and its only real policy tool was the "hammer": shutting down state funding, announcing austerity measures, along with a political crackdown. When growth was too fast, the hammer came down. When growth and its accompanying problems subsided, the hammer was raised. Since the early 1990s, the hammer has shrunk in size and found alternative ways of expressing itself, less through political and more through macro-economic methods. The man of the hour behind these economic policy changes has been Zhu Rongji, a former mayor of Shanghai and a vice-premier of China's State Council as well as a member of the Politburo Standing Committee.

Stage I 1976–84: Getting started

Having just returned to power following the fall of the Gang of Four and the end of the Cultural Revolution, Deng initiated decentralisation of economic planning and put China on the path of reform. Like Mao Zedong before him, Deng proved a revolutionary, a politician and an economic reformer all in one.

The first measures included the creation of five SEZs, with Shenzhen being the largest, so as to act as experimental areas for a Chinese market economy to take shape. Communes were de-collectivised and the responsibility system was instituted, with the primary focus being reform of the agriculture system. In industry, state-owned enterprises were allowed to retain their profits. In 1984, the People's Bank of China (PBOC) was established as the central bank, the former commercial banking activities of the bank being injected into a newly organised commercial bank, the Industrial and Commercial Bank of China (ICBC).

On the political front, this period of initializing the market economy went through a rough spot during the 1979 border war with Vietnam and the Democracy Wall Movement, which, in some circles, became identified with a challenge to Deng. GNP growth averaged 8.8% during the period.

Stage II 1985–87: Full steam ahead

With success in the countryside came the extension of the reform process to the urban areas in 1984. Enterprise reform went into full swing with the implementation of enterprise taxation, wage reform, and a new banking system. In 1986, foreign exchange swap centres were set up and the contract responsibility system was extended from agriculture to enterprises. The end of the period experienced a backlash against market-driven growth and by 1987 conservatives managed to have Hu Yaobang step down from the post of general secretary of the Chinese Communist Party, a post he had held since 1978. Zhao Ziyang, who had held the post of premier, was appointed in Hu's place and Li Peng was named to replace Zhao. GNP growth averaged 10.6% during the period.

Stage III 1988–90: Conservatism and crackdown

Following more than a decade of rapid change, conservatives initiated a number of campaigns against "spiritual pollution" to remind people that China could only go so far in taking up Western ways. In late 1988 and early 1989, retail inflation moved above 25% and the natural response was to re-centralise the economy. The message was most clearly conveyed following the Tiananmen crackdown in June 1989. The June 4 crackdown had followed a summer of active demonstrations across the country and the mourning of the death of former general secretary Hu Yaobang in April. For his perceived role in condoning the student movement, Zhao Ziyang was reported to have been placed under house arrest only days before the crackdown. Less than a month later he was stripped of all posts and Jiang Zemin, then mayor of Shanghai, was appointed general secretary in his place.

Besides the student and worker protests there was also the fact that national inflation had been running above 25% during the first quarter of 1989. The entire country was on edge and was ready for a period of consolidation. Re-centralisation of the economy in 1989 seemed almost a natural response. GNP growth averaged 6.5% during the period.

Stage IV 1991–95: Recovery, boom and pullback

In the aftermath of Tiananmen Square, China underwent a subdued 18 months while being shunned by the international community. This stage was in fact also allowing China to prepare for a new wave of liberalisations such as the world has seldom seen. The call to action, of course, came from Deng Xiaoping following his *nanxun*, or southern tour of inspection, to Guangdong in the winter of 1992.

Across the country, prices on hundreds of items were allowed to follow the laws of supply and demand. From steel to grain, prices rose to near those of the outside world. With building materials in strong demand during 1993, key materials such as glass and cement, for instance, even rose above world price levels. By mid-1993, grain prices had been decontrolled in 80% of the country.

What followed the price liberalisation of 1992 was a powerful two-year economic boom throughout coastal regions and SEZs that ended only a few months after a "maximum bullish" signal on China was sent out by Morgan Stanley, a US investment house, in late 1993. The market forces let loose in 1992 were so powerful that many indicators of growth continued to register strong gains for more than a year after China's economic policy strongman and vice premier, Zhu Rongji, launched a 16-point programme to cool down the economy in July 1993. In 1994, as in late 1988 and early 1989, inflation once again approached 25%. This time, however, price inflation remained stubbornly high for a longer period, partly as result of runaway food prices. Nearly a year after the government had re-imposed price controls on key items, inflation figures fell magically to the 15% target set earlier in the year. GNP growth for the period 1991–95 averaged 11.6%.

Conclusion

A nagging issue inhibiting the development of fully-fledged corporations in China has been a lackadaisical attitude toward the maximisation of profit as it is known in mature and some newly-industrialised economies. Needing further improvement are the corporate structures of leading groups such that they may grow to resemble their cousins in Taiwan and Singapore. Taking a few more lessons from MNCs operating in China would also prove beneficial. Over the next five to ten years, growth at top companies is likely to remain somewhat directionless. That is, companies will grow in the direction of least resistance, with little regard to adhering to corporate codes. China's challenge is none other than to deepen the restructuring of its companies along basic market principles.

Putting aside the hard reality that China to date has few, if any, world-class corporations, post-revolution China has travelled up the learning curve rapidly as compared to the days of Soviet-style economic planning under veteran economist Chen Yun (who died in April 1995). China has also grown beyond its economic experiments in the five principal SEZs, set up under the aegis of Deng after 1979. Since 1991, a key force behind spectacular growth in the economy is continued liberalisation of the private sector. One major boost in 1992 was an across-the-board price liberalisation of major products. This, combined with a symbolic green light for growth given by Deng in Shenzhen in early 1992, put China's growth into overdrive for the next two to three years. Economic consolidation during the mid-1990s offered a breather to China's inflation-burdened consumers.

Appendices

Appendix 1A: Chronology of events 1976–97

1976	
January	Death of Zhou Enlai
April	Deng Xiaoping barred from all work
September	Mao Zedong dies
1977	
July	Third Plenum of Third Party Congress. Deng restored to Politburo
August	Eleventh Party Congress. Hua Guofeng praises Mao
1978	
December	Third Plenum of Eleventh Party Congress pushes through the "Four Modernisations" Politburo meeting appoints Hu Yaobang as party secretary
1979	
January	Deng encourages Democracy Wall movement
February	China attacks Vietnamese positions
September	Fourth Plenum of Eleventh Party Congress puts Zhao Ziyang in Politburo
1980	
February	Hu and Zhao are promoted to Politburo Standing Committee
August	Enlarged Politburo meeting replaces Hua Guofeng as Premier with Zhao
November	Deng put in control of Central Military Commission
1981	
March	Deng first mentions "Struggle against bourgeois liberalism"
June	Hu named party chairman
December	Chen Yun criticises Hu
1982	
January	Hu calls for using foreign capital in China's liberalisation drive
August	At Seventh Plenum of Party Congress Hua criticises "practice as the sole criterion of truth"

Appendix 1A: Chronology of events 1976–97

September	Twelfth Party Congress opens, Chen Yun faction launches attack against "bourgeois liberalism", post of party chairman abolished
1983	
January	Hu and Deng Liqun debate the role of ideology and politics in China's modernisation
1984	
February	Deng tours south; heated debate on SEZs among leadership
April	Politburo meeting recognises importance of SEZs, opens more
1985	
January	Deng's *Building Socialism with Chinese Characteristics* is published
September	Chen Yun criticises party members for straying from ideals of communism
1986	
December	Hu criticised by Deng for his handling of party intellectuals
1987	
January	Hu relieved of duties as party general secretary
October	Zhao appointed acting general secretary
November	Li Peng named acting premier; Zhao elected general secretary
1988	
March	Seventh NPC approves Li Peng as premier. Yang Shangkun is named president
April	Hainan is granted status of province
1989	
April	Death of Hu; students begin to occupy Tiananmen Square
May	Zhao reported to be under house arrest
June	Tiananmen crackdown; Jiang appointed party general secretary at Fourth Plenum of Thirteenth Party Congress. Zhao is officially stripped of all posts

Appendix 1A: Chronology of events 1976–97

1990	
March	Li Peng strikes austere tone at Third Session of Seventh NPC
April	Jiang appointed to Central Military Commission chair
1991	
April	Zhu Rongji and Zou Jiahua appointed as vice-premiers
1992	
January	Deng makes his famous *nanxun* to southern provinces and calls for more economic reforms
October	Fourteenth Party Congress establishes basis of China's "socialist market economy". Central Advisory Commission chaired by Chen Yun is abolished. Yang Shangkun and many associates are purged
December	Zhu gives the first orders to slow down the economy
1993	
March	Eighth NPC names Jiang as president and Rong Yiren vice-president. Zhu becomes executive vice-premier in charge of the economy
July	Zhu puts forth 16-point programme to slow the economy and takes over as governor of the PBOC
1994	
September	Shanghai mayor Huang Ju is made a Politburo member at the Fourth Plenum of the Central Committee meeting
October	Zhu's duties seen curtailed in favour of Jiang associates. Parts of current portfolio are given to Wu Bangguo and Jiang Chunyun
1995	
March	Third session of Eighth NPC confirms meteoric rise of Wu Bangguo with election to the post of vice-premier in charge of industry. Jiang Chunyun is also confirmed as the new vice-premier in charge of agriculture, but not without opposition

Appendix 1A: Chronology of events 1976–97

December	Victories over inflation are claimed as the government falls within its 15% target. Zhu Rongji quietly re-establishes his influence following recent appointments of his supporters in areas such as the China Securities Regulatory Commission
1996	
January	Inflation falls to the 10% level for the first time since 1992. Share prices for locals begin to rally
June	First major rally for foreigner shares hits Shenzhen
October	Zhou Beifang receives a suspended death sentence for taking and giving bribes while a senior executive of Shougang Steel's Hong Kong subsidiary
1997	
February	Deng dies. Following a state funeral, specifically excluding black sheep such as Deng Liqun and Zhao Ziyang, Deng's ashes are scattered across the South China Sea. Jiang considered the "core" of the party leadership
September	15th Party Congress confirms Jiang as heir to Deng Xiaoping, as well as Zhu Rongji's rise to the #3 spot in the party. Both Jiang and Zhu are seen as allied in the task of reforming the SOEs. Retail inflation falls to zero

Appendix 1B: A summary of China's economy in graphs

1.1: Foreign exchange reserves, debt, direct investment

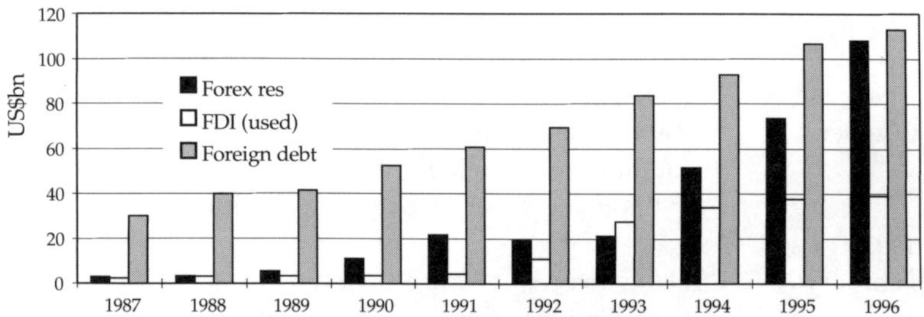

Sources: China Statistical Yearbook, 1996; World Bank; consensus estimates

1.2: Growth of GNP, inflation, industry, CPI

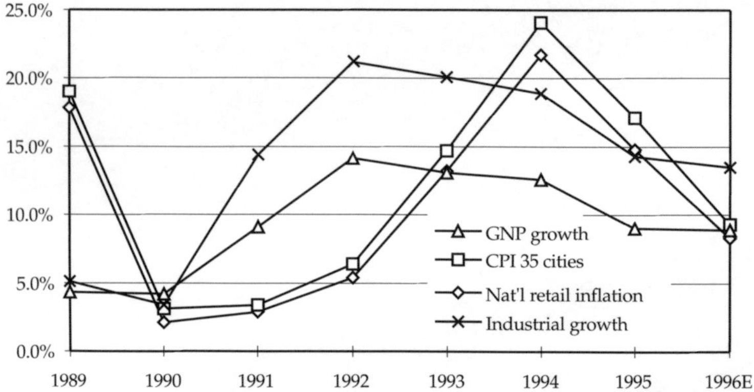

Source: China Statistical Yearbook, 1996

1.3: Growth of exports and imports

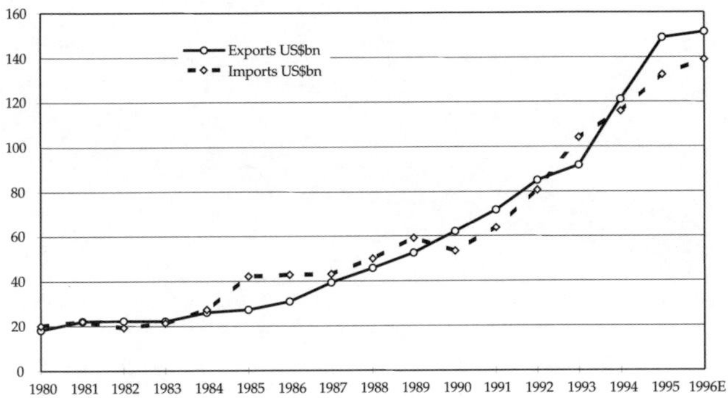

Source: China Statistical Yearbook, 1996

CHAPTER 2

The growth of China's key conglomerates

Charles de Trenck

There are ten or more major state-backed companies which can be said to be independent companies. The companies bear distinctive management styles and reputations with the outside business world and include such names as CITIC, China Resources, China Merchants, COSCO, CNNC, Top Glory (China CEROIL Food), Guangdong Enterprises, Shougang, and a few others. A number of China's top banks have also developed independent management structures, including the Bank of China, Bank of Communications and the Industrial and Commercial Bank of China (ICBC). However, the banking sector remains tightly controlled within China.

Of the companies and banks holding foreign currency debt instruments, Moody's and other credit rating agencies have since 1994 moved to issue ratings separate from China's sovereign rating. The shift in ratings policy reflects the perceived separation of these firms from the protective mantle of the state. This separation is more often than not only skin deep. On the one hand, these firms exhibit distinct management styles that result in different profitability and debt levels. On the other hand, most of the key decisions are still made in accordance with the wishes of controlling government bodies.

Alphabet soup: What is a red chip?

Our own focus here is on companies with listings, or control over listed vehicles. These companies invite only two major categories, those which are incorporated and listed in Hong Kong, usually termed red chips, and those which are incorporated in China but listed on overseas markets, usually labelled with the first letter of the market in which they are listed (currently H for Hong Kong and N for New York). Shares listed in China and open to foreign investors are labelled with the letter B.

The characteristics that differentiate a red chip from an H or an N (or even a B) share are constantly confused. Press and brokerage reports will from time to time consider H shares or shares of "China concept" (see below) companies to fall under a general category of "red chips". Red chips, on the other hand, are never labelled as H shares, indicating that red chips are considered, in this loose definition, as including all China shares. The loose definition of red chips could not be more wrong.

The class of shares that depends on China operations for growth, but is not backed by a Chinese business or government entity, is usually labelled as China concept. Taking the point to its extreme, one could find a China concept stock, say one owned by an Overseas Chinese family from Thailand, to be more exposed to China than a red chip. In the early years of red chips, the early 1990s, such a case was not uncommon, since their holding companies initially injected their Hong Kong investments.

Strictly speaking, red chips are extensions of governmental organisations operating within investment and cash-raising guidelines laid down by a holding company and a controlling government body. H or N shares represent specific assets, usually a collection of factories, and are chips off the block of selected state enterprises around China. Red chips have sought listings in Hong Kong, sometimes with and sometimes without government consent, and have grown through a consistent pattern of acquisitions. Red chips that did not seek formal approval from supervising bodies typically have gained their listing in Hong Kong through a back-door entry into an inactive listed company. H or N shares were selected for listing by securities authorities in consultations with Beijing and provincial organisations. Some red chips gained their listings as early as the late 1980s, whereas H and N shares saw their first listings in 1993.

What does a red chip conglomerate do?

A red chip conglomerate is something of a midwife for the parent: it facilitates the transfer of assets from a government-backed entity to the equity markets. The assets transferred typically represent the most profitable among the group. Such acquisitions are usually considered related-party transactions. Additional assets are also made available from organisations holding various degrees of affinity with a red chip. Take the case of the Guangdong Ministry of Power's relationship to Guangdong Investment (GDI). GDI's parent is owned by the Guangdong government, but the Ministry of Power operates independently of Guangdong Enterprises and any power generation asset acquired from the province is through an arm's-length transaction.

Some critics have raised concerns over the practice of asset swapping from parent to listed company. But most Chinese authorities have condoned these activities. In the end, they have no reason not to approve, since prices paid by equity investors are substantial — and control remains in the hands of the same government entity. Red chips have proven to be popular with investors because they provide an income base diverse in both geographic and industry distribution. Earnings have thus been less volatile.

What do H, B or N shares do?

H or N shares represent plays on individual industries. Generally, income is restricted to a few factories that have recently upgraded their production capacity. Sales are generated in large part within China. The factories listed typically represent enterprises that are close to the top in their industries. The very best, such as Baoshan Steel near Shanghai, were left off lists during the first few selections. However, listing the best and newest equipped firms was not excluded either, as in the case of Yizheng Chemical Fibre.

Reversal of fortune

These industrials, with the exception of a few companies, have seen their share prices trade at significant discounts to those of red chips. The cause of the underperformance was a collapse that followed on the heels of a buying frenzy in late 1993. Not one of the "alphabet soup" companies escaped the carnage inflicted by foreign investors in 1994 and 1995.

After a series of startling profit drops for H, N and B shares beginning with interim results in mid-1994, being classified under a letter category became an invitation for ridicule in the international investment community. In investors' eyes, these companies had misrepresented their earnings/growth potential and were incapable of carrying out any coherent long-term investment strategy, such as coordinated new plant investment as detailed in listing prospectuses. Not only were China's macro-economic belt-tightening measures affecting earnings growth, but these companies had simply hoodwinked investors and won excessive listing valuations. Funds raised from the listings were simply misspent or idling in Hong Kong bank deposits taking currency exchange losses while the renminbi strengthened.

The international investment community was flabbergasted by continued negative revelations on H shares throughout 1994 and 1995. What made the experience all the more painful for them was that the growth story had been swallowed hook, line and sinker during the second half of 1993. During this period, H shares such as Shanghai Petrochem and Tsingtao Brewery outperformed Hong Kong's own powerful rally.

Sentiment became so negative toward these share classes in 1995 that more than a dozen planned listings were postponed or cancelled. Though morale had recovered somewhat by early 1996, it was in this environment during the mid-1990s that red chips came to be seen as offering a relative safe haven.

The road to establishing a conglomerate

There are three general characteristics state-backed companies have in common. First, their authority devolves from the State Council, a government ministry under the State Council, or a regional government. Second, they typically have established Hong Kong incorporated subsidiaries with an additional subsidiary listed on the Hong Kong Stock Exchange. And third, they engage in complex assets for debt or equity swaps with the international investment community, usually through their Hong Kong subsidiary. The injections arising from these complex swaps leave a wide trail of investments across industries, turning these companies into sprawling mini-conglomerates with little regard for the bottom line, particularly at the holding company level. The scattered nature of these investments often leads investors to question the experience of management of these companies. Growth often is not so much strategic as it is for the sake of capital and expansion!

The process of growing these state-backed companies out of international capital began in the early 1980s. During the early 1990s the deal flow became a torrent. Deng's tour through Guangdong in winter 1992 was a green light to would-be capitalists, and shortly thereafter a rush for Hong Kong's property and stock market followed.

To calculate how much international capital has been spent for stakes in China assets or for indirect participations in project financing by Hong Kong–listed arms of China-backed companies would require a painstaking roll call of major international banks (in addition to the easy part of adding up equity issues). A rough estimate of funds raised from equity and debt financing for these transactions stands in the range of US$40–60bn, or 20 to 30 times the 1995 year-end market capitalisation of Hong Kong listed H shares (Hong Kong listed China industrials specifically selected by Chinese authorities). This rough calculation amounts to about one-half of China's official foreign borrowings.

The Xinhua news agency, on 3 July 1996, said that China has set up 4,800 companies in 130 countries, with total investment amounting to US$5.5bn. Not counted in these figures was a more detailed accounting of the amounts invested back in China by foreign-incorporated subsidiaries of mainland companies.

Understanding how funds are raised and invested

China-backed firms in Hong Kong have set up very substantial banking facilities with, in addition to Chinese banks, Western banks, which during most of the 1980s and the early 1990s, were falling over each other to offer attractive financing arrangements. During this period, Japanese banks were more than happy to join in the free-for-all, making the spreads on the loans all the more unrealistic.

Tallying project finance loans, long- and short-term loans extended to Hong Kong subsidiaries of Chinese companies such as CITIC Hong Kong (Holdings), which is the subsidiary of CITIC Beijing and the controlling shareholder of Hong Kong-listed CITIC

Pacific, would require a gargantuan effort focused on identifying the process by which Chinese firms invest borrowed funds in China. A point to note is that funds borrowed overseas in this manner typically enter China as "foreign investment" and do not go down in the books as part of the total external debt held by China, which at end-year 1994 stood at US$97bn according to the World Bank. According to Business Monitor International, China's external debt stood at US$100.5bn in 1994 and US$110.4bn in 1995.

If the funds raised do not go back to China as investment, their next favourite home is either Hong Kong property or the stock market. Where the funds go and whether funds are used effectively depends on the group. CITIC Hong Kong (Holdings), for instance, has developed a solid reputation for expert management of its investments. Many other smaller conglomerates, however, indiscriminately invest in deals they come across (often from the parent), without asking themselves whether there is a fit with their stated corporate strategy (if there is one at all) or if the deal is all that profitable.

Behind the ratings game

Funds raised through loans by Chinese companies in Hong Kong are often not included as part of China's debt because the funds are forwarded by foreign banks on an unsecured or "clean" basis. Moreover, China does not issue specific guarantees for the debt of these companies and the China holding companies of these subsidiaries could be expected to offer only moral support in case of default. This issue was made clearer in mid-1995 following downgrades by Moody's on the debt ratings of a number of companies. For instance, the rating on Guangdong Enterprises was reduced from Baa3, the lowest investment grade rating, to Ba1 in May 1995. A Ba1 rating is considered one level below the lowest investment grade rating, or the highest rating for a "junk bond". As with a similar downgrade of Guangdong International Trust and Investment Corp (GITIC) to Baa2 from Baa1, Moody's was decoupling provincially-backed entities from Beijing-backed entities, such as CITIC.

However, a case could be made that the balance sheets of most Chinese institutions have been weak right from the start, that

Beijing in fact never really provided guarantees on the debt of most quasi-government backed organisations and that these downgrades should have been made far earlier. One could argue that the ratings should have begun from a lower base because of weak fundamentals and should have been upgraded selectively following a slow improvement in the managerial practices and the balance sheets of some of these companies.

Moody's downgrades on Chinese corporate debt in 1995 followed its own improved coverage of these companies and a shift in sentiment in the market place following a few high-profile losses in derivatives trading from subsidiaries of leading Chinese companies. Some of the more prominent names involved included Minmetals International Non-Ferrous Metals, Sinochem USA and CITIC Shanghai. The mini-scandals in derivatives, however, represented more a problem of weak credit reviews on the part of foreign banks that did not put enough attention into identifying subsidiaries within groups separately. It appears that lines approved for use by the parent and for certain companies within a group came to be used under conditions that were separate from their original intent. In some of the cases, insufficient attention was paid to treating a specific subsidiary as a different credit risk from the parent. Insufficient attention was paid as well to specific individuals trading within subsidiaries.

One documented case of approved facilities that may have been abused which appeared in the press is that of Lehman Brothers' encounter with a Hong Kong company under the name of Senior Market. The company had as one of its directors a former deputy general manager of a company under Sinochem and was alleged to have funnelled some of its trading profits to a British Virgin Islands company under its control. The Hong Kong company later became one of the centres of attention in US$20mn of losses registered by Sinochem in late 1993 and early 1994, and suits and counter-suits filed by Lehman and Sinochem respectively.

Moody's said a reason for its downgrades was a move by China's Ministry of Finance to issue debt on the international markets directly rather than only through leading state-backed companies. Following this move, certain credit-rating institutions knocked on doors requesting letters of guarantee from Beijing for many of the leading companies and banks which had issued international paper. The state was only willing to provide letters of comfort, which for bankers represent only an expression of moral support and not a legal document promising reimbursement of funds in case of default by a borrowing institution. Although Beijing had never formally issued guarantee letters, Moody's felt that the degree of backing from the state had lessened.

Adding up the numbers

Specific project loans executed on behalf of a company incorporated in China requires approval, usually from the State Administration of Exchange Control (SAEC). Foreign partners can no longer receive such guarantees from Chinese partners, so access to guarantees is strictly limited to the China-risk portion of a project. Four designated banks: the Bank of China, the Industrial and Commercial Bank of China, the People's Construction Bank of China, and the Agricultural Bank of China, are generally allowed to give the go ahead for China party loans by means of issuing guarantees on the specific projects to the foreign banks making the loans. If other banks are involved, they must first receive approval from the SAEC. Loans approved under SAEC authority have been included in China's external debt calculations. Also included in such calculations are loans granted to CITIC Beijing.

Is everything on the balance sheet?

A key issue in evaluating overall debt levels, however, is the question of the degree of consolidation of accounts. For listed subsidiaries of groups there are typically no red flags waved with respect to reported accounts. Listed red chips are, by and large, good corporate citizens. However, there can at times be somewhat of a grey area as regards the accounts of their parents. It is not unusual to see qualifications from the auditors to the effect that accounts — and therefore liabilities — have not been fully consolidated.

A banker can never be quite sure of how large grey areas on the balance sheet actually are. This is highlighted by the fact that some of the groups that come up for scrutiny somehow never quite consolidate all their accounts, leaving the auditors' report with a long list of qualifications to their opinions. "We have not been able to satisfy ourselves as to the nature of/recoverability of/carrying value of ..." often pervade the auditors' report. We note one example of the 1992 accounts from Guangdong Enterprises. In the 1993 auditor's report four major items were flagged as not being consolidated in the accounts. By the time the 1993 accounts were generated, the 1992 accounts had been completely restated and the net assets of the group reduced significantly (see Chapter 7 on Guangdong Enterprises).

Of misdirected investments and cheap funding

Where have the funds raised in equity and debt issues gone? Have the funds been used efficiently? These were the first questions lenders and investors asked when in late 1993 and early 1994 it became apparent that China was settling in to a high-inflation, lower-economic-growth environment. Funds raised from H share issues were partially invested in upgrading capacity and partly left idling in bank deposits. A significant portion of the projects are not earnings-enhancing for these state corporations. The more attractive ones are invested in by specialised direct investment funds. More significantly, the industrial investments held by these companies have yielded low returns over the last several years. Yet, state-backed companies are charged with the mission of building up China's industry and infrastructure.

In 1995, when few equity investors wanted to be seen having funds placed in China equities, some of the harsher critics pointed to companies such as Tsingtao Brewery as examples of companies that had squandered the funds they had raised from international investors. The criticism levelled at Tsingtao was that it had taken funds earmarked for investment in new capacity and re-invested them as high-interest-bearing loans to other companies. Though one of the more celebrated cases of inappropriate usage of funds, it was assumed that many of the other listed Chinese firms were engaging in the same practices. After all, it could be argued that relending funds at rates above 15% could offer a reasonable return on capital.

These concerns were to a certain extent over-blown given China's double-digit inflation environment during the mid-1990s. After placing bank deposits with Chinese institutions it might be considered natural to want that extra return by having the bank loan out the funds for a few months at a time for a higher rate of return than a standard bank deposit. With lending policies kept tight to deal with inflationary pressures, the cost of capital was driven up and money lending became a profit centre for cash-rich H shares that were themselves psyched out by China's credit environment. Though not ideal from a long-term investment perspective, a company such as Tsingtao could tell itself that re-lending the funds at double-digit rates could earn more than investing in a new plant, confounding equity investors who thought they were accessing instant capacity growth in the beer market, not the money market! But in China's economic environment of the mid-1990s it was understandable.

The difference between Hong Kong and mainland cost of capital
The importance of obtaining funds in Hong Kong can not be emphasised enough because the cost of long-term capital in international markets for companies with a good credit standing is typically around LIBOR/HIBOR (London/Hong Kong interbank offered rate) + 0.5–1.0%. The economic environment of the mid-1990s thus put the cost of capital in the 6.0–8.0% range. Across the border in China the cost of capital was 15–25% during the same period. The official rate quoted by banks has been closer to 10% but few organisations have had access to much capital at this "concessionary rate".

Though some may view an interest rate differential between Hong Kong and China as only a short term distortion from efficient market forces, which should dictate an immediate increase in the cost of capital to adjust for China risk, and where the 1997 handover would also see a redefinition of ratings for Hong Kong borrowings, it could be argued that Hong Kong has become China's foremost offshore centre with an efficient financial market and convertibility for the currency underpinning the lower-cost capital.

The major stipulation for Chinese enterprises accepted by both China and foreign parties is that in order for a Chinese group to qualify for access to a lower-cost capital, a group must be in possession of a company incorporated outside China. The question of whether funds ultimately are shifted to China does not appear to be a major issue — though it should be.

1997 and the cost of capital

The issue of borrowing at a lower cost and shifting the funds to China will likely invite additional scrutiny after 1997. This is because Hong Kong authorities will have to fight harder with international lending bodies to differentiate Hong Kong risk from China risk. An AP-Dow Jones report, 25 June 1996, for instance, followed up on new regulations issued by the State Administration of Exchange Control on 16 April 1996. The regulations effectively cap overseas borrowing of Chinese banks' foreign subsidiaries and prohibit the repatriation of foreign exchange raised overseas. The new regulations were issued, and repeated in June, following the voicing of concerns by bodies such as the Hong Kong Monetary Authority that Chinese banks could flood the Hong Kong and world market with debt-raising issues. A flood of such issues could drive up borrowing costs for Hong Kong companies. As pointed out elsewhere in the current discussion, it does not appear that similar guidelines have been set for Chinese enterprises incorporated in Hong Kong. A 23 October 1996 article in the *South China Morning Post* confirmed fears of a squeeze on borrowers beyond 1997 when it pointed out that Hong Kong companies had raised 56% more cash via the debt markets in the first nine months of 1996 compared to the same period in 1995. The companies borrowed US$15.9bn in the first nine months of 1996. The rise was attributed to companies building up their reserves in case it became harder to borrow funds after the 1997 handover.

An argument can be made that, even after the return of Hong Kong to China in July 1997, a large differential between the cost of capital in Hong Kong and on the mainland remains likely. The differential will be maintained as a result of Hong Kong's continued status as an offshore financial centre under the new SAR government, to serve China's thirst for capital to fuel growth across the border. Were China not to maintain this distinction between the cost of capital in Hong Kong and China, its cheapest source of funding would evaporate, creating an entirely new set of worries for Beijing.

In concluding that a substantial differential in the cost of capital will be maintained, however, it is also clear that the issue of a potential devaluation in the Hong Kong dollar and a subsequent jump in interest rates will remain a concern of the capital markets. It would not be unreasonable to expect a certain narrowing of the differential in the cost of capital between Hong Kong and China after 1997.

Confusing the short and long term

On the level of analysing individual firms and their capital management habits, and of greater practical concern to lenders has been the practice among Chinese companies to engage in the mismatching of short-term liabilities with long-term or higher risk investments. One could go so far as to claim that this practice has been encouraged by the lending international banks as a result of a good-faith attempt to build up their China business.

Foreign lending institutions, competing amongst each other for lead roles, want to gain Brownie points with the China parent of the Hong Kong subsidiary. Since trade finance is profitable and low risk for banks, an attempt is made to win over some trade finance from these firms. However trade finance facilities are often bundled with short-term loan facilities, and inevitably the Chinese firms go for the short-term loan and ignore the trade finance facility. When a Hong Kong subsidiary of a China conglomerate operates a dozen subsidiaries in Hong Kong, the amounts borrowed on a short-term basis, and often rolled over on a continuous basis, can be quite substantial. A glance at the balance sheets of most subsidiaries of state-backed companies in the territory will attest to this.

For Chinese-backed firms, the advantage of borrowing over the short term is that the cost can be more than 120 basis points less than the cost of longer-term capital, or HIBOR/LIBOR + 0.40–0.70% (long-term funds can easily cost HIBOR/LIBOR + 120–200 basis points). With this cheap source of funding, the Hong Kong holding is able to shift funds into financing working capital needs of subsidiaries back in China (such as accounts receivable that would be more likely to face higher provisions for bad debts), play the stock or property markets with greater freedom, or invest the funds as capital destined for long-term investment.

How to build and operate a Chinese conglomerate with a listed red chip

Mainland Chinese companies have established their own particular genre, often dictated by the assets they acquire. An ornate group-holding structure has become a tried and tested means to establishing an overseas presence. Company after company has followed the path to incorporating a subsidiary in Hong Kong and proceeding to acquire companies and assets both on the mainland and in Hong Kong. First capital is borrowed from foreign banks, and when the holding structure is more established, funds are raised on the equity markets by way of listing and further injections (see figure 2.1).

2.1: The injection machine

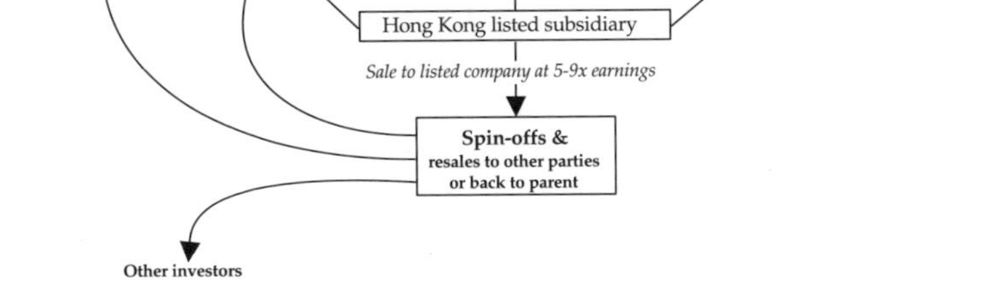

Generic listing model

The standard approach of a mainland firm making its move for expansion and overseas capital has been to: first, establish a Hong

Kong subsidiary; second, borrow funds from banks to finance existing operations of subsidiaries and associates; and third, find a way to gain listing in Hong Kong (see figure 2.2).

2.2: Generic model for government-related conglomerates

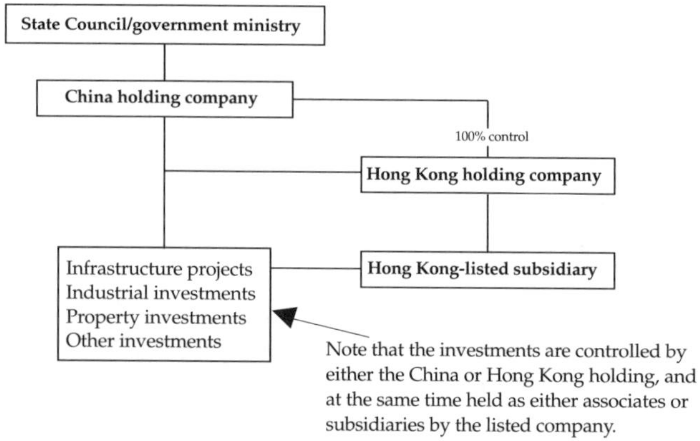

The road to raising capital for China assets is long and drawn out. With H share listings, Beijing's watchful eye monitors the valuations for the assets of the new company through the auspices of the State Asset Bureau. The discipline established by the practice has prevented fire sales of China's assets, though it has also raised questions with some investors when they have been confronted with buying into outdated equipment. For state-backed companies in Hong Kong, valuations and acquisitions have been more flexible. If there is difficulty buying a significant stake, a small associate stake is first acquired and then upgraded at a propitious time.

Some red chips have sought the approval of the State Council. This is usually considered a necessity for assets held at the national level and that are above US$30mn. China Resources, for instance, sought approval for the acquisition of a US$44mn stake in a Beijing property company in November 1994. But many acquisitions are smaller and do not require Beijing's approval. Logically, therefore, it might be considered easier to initiate a number of smaller transactions over a period of time, than to go for an acquisition all at once. Up to 1995, this pattern of seeking smaller stakes or smaller investments initially was practiced by a number of investors, including foreign and Chinese companies established overseas for the purpose of investing in China. Then, in 1995, Beijing began to crack down on those engaged in this practice.

Property investments

The main diversion for Chinese enterprises in Hong Kong and in China has been aggressive expansion into property investment and development in Hong Kong. Chinese conglomerates invariably create a number of companies and subsidiaries upon arrival in Hong Kong. Key parts of the group then proceed to draw up plans to invest in property, often projects in Hong Kong and a city in China from which they originate. A group such as China National Non-ferrous Metals (CNNC), therefore, will set up shop in Hong Kong and plan for a large complex in Beijing. Next, such a group moves to distribute its exposure to the project through apportioning parts of the assets and future assets (therefore also liabilities) to various subsidiaries. In 1994, Chinese firms accounted for about 30% of the property transaction volume in Hong Kong. In the first 11 months of 1995 these firms accounted for about 16% of transactions, reflecting more subdued buying from Chinese following continued austerity in China. A rebound in investment by these firms is a foregone conclusion. A new wave of eager investors from China in 1997 is expected to reverse the trend experienced in 1995.

Appendices

Appendix 2A:Leading conglomerates

BEIJING ENTERPRISES	
Listed flagship:	Beijing Enterprises Holdings Ltd
Listed since:	1997
Principal activities:	Tourism; hotel management, brewery and fast-food operations, toll road operations

Hands down, Beijing Enterprises, under the Beijing municipal governments unlisted company, Beijing Holdings Ltd (formerly Scriven Trading Ltd), has shot to the pinnacle of the charts among red chips. One year prior to the May 1997 listing, investors would have shrugged their shoulders showing complete ignorance of the company. In May, its Hong Kong IPO was 1,276x oversubscribed, surpassing the 892x level clocked by GITIC Enterprises, the building materials division of Guangdong's largest international trust, in March 1997. What moved investors, particularly retail investors, to break all records were images of unbeatable concepts such as the Great Wall and the Beijing McDonalds chain included within the listing. Listing the Great Wall (the Badaling section of the Wall northwest of Beijing to be exact), as some observers may want to look back upon the event, conjures up the most powerful image of what red chips stand for during China's continued experiment with market liberalisation.

Based on an IPO price of HK$12.48, the company's fully diluted listing price to earnings ratio was 19.4x its forecast 1997 earnings, already considered among the highest listing ratios in Hong Kong. But with the unofficial grey market price (before the start of official trade) having been reported as high as HK$48, and given the first day close of trading of the share price at HK$40.20, the effective price to earnings ratio *paid* by investors put the ratio closer to a range of 60–77x 1997 earnings. Following the previously unparalleled success of Shanghai Industrial following its listing in May 1996, investors decided that they would bid up the company's share price all at once, as opposed to the Shanghai cousin, Shanghai Industrial, that had seen its share price multiply by a factor of four within the space of one year. In bidding the share price up by about a factor of four before official trading even began, investors were pre-empting the same style of injections seen among red chips during 1996–97. In the case of Beijing Enterprises, investors expected such injections as key utilities projects in Beijing to be injected later in 1997 and in 1998.

CHINA AEROSPACE

Listed flagship:	China Aerospace
Controlled since:	1992
Principal activities:	TV manufacturing, electronics, automotive

The group, whose Beijing parent, China Aerospace Corp. (CASC), oversees functions in aerospace and defense. It controls or oversees more than 300 research centres and three universities. CASC's arrival in Hong Kong in 1992 led the way for speculation in China-backed companies when it acquired control in the ailing Hong Kong–listed Conic Investment. The TV manufacturer was bleeding red ink when China Aerospace arrived on the scene and turned the company's operations around within a year.

The major purpose for the group's arrival in Hong Kong has been to develop high-technology products for distribution in China. To this end, China Aerospace is building a science park in the Guangdong district of Huizhou. Another key investment was a purchase from the parent of light-truck manufacturing plants. Unfortunately, the truck production is of middling quality and turned in a low profitability rate during China's economic pullback in 1994–95. Another misguided investment appears to be the group's over-emphasis on TV manufacturing. Initial plans in 1994 called for substantial capital expenditures in medium- to high-end TV production, just as it became clear that the industry was in the midst of a collapse in margins.

CHINA CEROIL FOOD

Listed flagship:	Top Glory International
Controlled since:	1992
Principal activities:	Property development, investment
Listed vehicle:	China Food Holdings
Controlled since:	1992
Principal activities:	Edible oil processing, flour milling, investments

China National Cereals, Oils & Foodstuffs Import & Export Corp (China Ceroil Food) is China's principal importer of grain, edible oils and other food products and has become China's second largest trading company. The group was formed in the early 1950s under MOFTEC. Today it has 13 divisions controlling 23 wholly-owned subsidiaries, which generated in 1994 over US$10bn in turnover. Ceroil Food now handles more than 2,000 import and export commodities. With China becoming more reliant on grain imports, the group is likely to occupy a more central position in maintaining an adequate grain supply. Yet at the same time, it has diversified into property development in Hong Kong and Beijing, as well as into insurance. Investments extend to plantations in southeast Asia, Beijing and Hong Kong property developments, hotels, shipping and transport services.

CHINA EVERBRIGHT

Listed flagship:	China Everbright IHD
Controlled since:	1993
Principal activities:	Retail; property; banking
Listed subsidiary:	China Everbright International
Controlled since:	1993
Principal activities:	Property; industrial investments; automotive
Listed subsidiary:	China Everbright Technology
Controlled since:	1993
Principal activities:	Appliance manufacturing

China Everbright group was set up in Hong Kong in 1983 by the State Council and was one of the first state-owned organs established in Hong Kong. A long-time sleeper in Hong Kong, the group came to life twice in the 1990s. After a slow start during the

1980s, the group returned to Hong Kong in the early 1990s ready to increase its exposure by making several back-door entries into Hong Kong listed companies, led by group Chairwoman Qiu Qing and Wang Yake, a director at the group level, CEO of China Everbright-IHD and managing director of China Everbright International (among other appointments). Wang Yake was removed, however, after charges of embezzlement were reported to have been made against him. Sent to replace him was Zhu Xiaohua, a former deputy governor of the PBOC and considered an ally of Zhu Rongji. Zhu Xiaohua initiated, in May 1997, a new wave of corporate transactions, including the purchase of a 7.7% stake in Hong Kong Telecom for HK$11.4bn. The move was believed to be on behalf of other Chinese entities, ultimately representing China's Ministry of Posts and Telecommunications and represented China Everbright's role as a senior representative of the State Council. Also in May 1997, Zhu Xiaohua initiated a move to transfer a 20% stake in China Everbright Bank from the Hong Kong holding company to China Everbright IHD. China Everbright Bank which during the 1990s grew into one of China's leading banks, with assets reported to be Rmb47.1bn in 1996. The Hong Kong group holding company is also known for holding a 20% interest in Hong Kong listed International Bank of Asia.

CHINA INTERNATIONAL TRUST AND INVESTMENT CORP (CITIC)

Listed flagship:	CITIC Pacific (controlled by CITIC (HK) Holdings)
Controlled since:	1990
Principal activities:	Diversified investments ranging from infrastructure projects to aviation
Listed investment:	Ka Wah Bank (controlled by CITIC Beijing)
Controlled since:	1986
Principal activities:	Retail banking
Listed vehicle:	Continental Mariner (Controlled by CITIC Development/ Poly Technologies)
Controlled since:	1992
Principal activities:	Property, other investments

China International Trust & Investment Corporation (CITIC) is by far the largest and most established of Chinese companies. It is fair to say that parts of the group offer the best management China has developed to date. It was founded by Shanghai-born and long-time businessman Rong Yiren in 1978/9 as a principal overseas investment vehicle and conduit for foreign capital and know-how into China. The group's assets went from Rmb30mn in 1978/9 to consolidated assets of Rmb166.7bn in 1995. There are 27 wholly-owned subsidiaries within the group, with CITIC Industrial Bank being the largest. The Bank is widely seen as a leading second-tier bank, with assets of over US$10.4bn in 1995. Bearing the highest profile among overseas investors are Hong Kong-based CITIC (HK) Holdings and CITIC Pacific, whose activities will be discussed further in later chapters.

CITIC is divided into two major groupings. The first grouping is that made up of the more well-known companies under CITIC (HK) Holdings, which are led by Larry Yung, Rong Yiren's son. The second, which includes China Poly Group, CITIC (HK) Branch and Continental Mariner is led by Wang Jun, the son of Wang Zhen, an old-guard general who died in 1993. Both Larry Yung and Wang Jun are seen as belonging to a group of business leaders known as "Red Princelings" *(Zhonggong Taizi).* The Red Princes and Princesses of China are the sons and daughters of senior Chinese leaders who have turned their backgrounds into business relationships. Readers are recommended to consult *Princes and Princesses of Red China* by Ho Pin and Gao Xin to understand the interaction between the old guard of the Chinese Communist Party and the activities of their children in the China of the 1980s and 1990s.

CHINA MERCHANTS

Listed flagship:	China Merchants Hai Hong
Listed since:	1992
Principal activities:	Shipping, marine paints, industrials, toll roads
Listed investment:	Union Bank
Controlled since:	1986
Principal activities:	Banking

The group, founded in 1872, answers to the Ministry of Communications (in Chinese the term refers to transport), has since 1979 had the principal responsibility of developing the Shekou industrial zone outside Shenzhen, which has amassed over HK$40bn in investments. Its current chairman is Li Yinfei, 53. The group operates over 400 subsidiaries, the most important being:

- China Merchants Shekou Industrial Zone
- China Merchants Steam Navigation Co
- China Merchants Godown, Wharf & Transport Co
- China Merchants Bank
- China Southern Glass
- Hoi Tung Marine
- Ming Wah Shipping

The group's roots are shipping and it continues to operate a number of fleets of bulk carriers and tankers. In addition to developing Shekou, China Merchants has spawned a number of businesses in Hong Kong, Shenzhen and Pudong. China Merchants' industrial investments are spread out across China. Some of the projects are joint efforts with foreign partners and have been successful. However, there are a number of invested companies the group holds little or no expertise in, and it has been known to stray in its investment strategy.

China Merchants Bank

One of the more successful companies under the group, China Merchants Bank, has grown aggressively on the back of its parent's diverse investments in industrial areas, particularly in the Shenzhen and Shanghai areas. In 1995, the bank extended Rmb43.7bn in loans and reported Rmb1.7bn in profit. Its return on average assets (ROAA) for 1995 was 3.1%, up from 2% in 1994. The Bank has benefited from Guangdong's huge leap in exports during the 1990s. It has launched a number of new products, including new bank cards, ATM terminals and telephone banking services. China Merchants Bank has also made forays into investment banking and booming share prices in Shenzhen boosted the bank's securities operations. In late 1996, the company was considered a potential listing candidate on the Hong Kong stock exchange in 1997, but Beijing's conservatism with regards to listing its banks kept this on the back burner.

China Southern Glass

One often cited investment is the group's guidance of China Southern Glass, a downstream glass processing company that has also added a strategy of swimming upstream into float glass production. China Southern Glass has set up a plant in Shekou to produce its own float glass using new technology that allows it to produce both ultra-thin and ultra-thick float glass using the same equipment. Its way has thus far been fraught with difficult issues such as how to implement this new float-glass technology while no leading glass producer in the world has yet accomplished this task (it was found to be uneconomical by leading Western firms). Short-term respite from troubles in the glass industry was obtained by the company from property investments and the fact that it was able to buy glass from upstream producers in 1996 at rock-bottom prices, allowing its downstream operations to maintain margins despite its longer term strategy to move upstream.

Other corporate activities

In early 1996 the group was looking to reorganise itself, with a principal purpose being to gain additional control over its managerial structures and finances. Also in mind is to re-jig the group's holdings and inject further assets into its listed subsidiary, China Merchants Hai Hong. The first major injection after the original listing was made with the purchase of ships and a stake in China Southern Glass, listed in Shenzhen (and controlled by the group). In mid-1996, the Hong Kong listed company spun off, in Singapore, its Ming Wah Shipping division, raising about US$31mn The division consists of five Aframax tankers and one

Capesize vessel. By early 1997, the group was engaging in a new wave of injections of stakes in China toll roads.

CHINA NATIONAL NON-FERROUS METALS (CNNC)

Listed flagship:	ONFEM Holdings
Controlled since:	1993
Principal activities:	Property development
Listed vehicle:	Oriental Metals
Listed since:	1994
Principal activities:	Non-ferrous metals trading
Listed vehicle:	Silver Grant
Controlled since:	1993
Principal activities:	Diversified investment activities
Listed vehicle:	Simsen Metals
Listed since:	1994
Principal activities:	Non-ferrous metals trading

The group, founded in 1983, engages in the trading and processing of non-ferrous metals and controls some 80% of China's market for non-ferrous metals. Under its control are some 239 companies employing over one million persons. Total assets in 1992 were above Rmb32bn. At the same time, as with so many other leading companies, it has diversified into property development.

Oriental Metals is left to deal mainly with the group's core trading businesses, while ONFEM holdings, in addition to non-ferrous metals trading and investments in industrial projects and mines, has diversified into property development and investment in Guangzhou, Shanghai and Hong Kong. Wu Jianchang, CNNC's president, is chairman of the Hong Kong–listed companies. As with Shougang, CNNC is a Deng-related group in that Wu Jianchang is a son-in-law of Deng Xiaoping.

CHINA OCEAN SHIPPING CO (COSCO)

Listed flagship:	COSCO Pacific (formerly Florens Group)
Listed since:	1994
Principal activities:	Container leasing, container terminal operation

COSCO is a late bloomer engaged in aggressive growth. Until two years ago, it ran China's largest fleet of ships from Beijing, Shanghai and Hong Kong in relative seclusion. The original Beijing company was set up in 1961 and Shanghai operations were only begun during the 1970s. In Hong Kong, however, ownership of some parts of the group can be traced back to the 1950s. Although there were at one point about 200 Hong Kong companies (one or a few ships held per company) controlled by the group, COSCO was known for operating two long-established Hong Kong shipping companies, Yick Fung and Ocean Tramping. COSCO is often thought of as a container vessel operator, but even today the group as a whole operates more bulk vessels than container ships. It is generally recognised that COSCO operates more than 600 vessels with a total tonnage of 17mn dwt worldwide, making the group one of the largest shipping companies in the world.

In August 1994 the group reorganised and incorporated its flagship Hong Kong subsidiary, COSCO (HK) Group Ltd, which paved the way for the listing of its container leasing subsidiary, Florens Group, in December of the same year on the Hong Kong stock exchange. COSCO reports to the Ministry of Communications, as does its cousin China Merchants.

In 1996, the group initiated its second major restructuring, mainly designed around a growing Hong Kong presence. COSCO (HK) holds the bulk of the investments in vessels, property, port and container developments, fleet management services, and holding of the container leasing subsidiary, Florens. COSCO Beijing, on the other hand, retains the management of a more than 150 container vessel fleet and interests in the majority of the China port development projects.

CHINA OVERSEAS HOLDINGS

Listed vehicle:	China Overseas Land
Listed since:	1992
Principal activities:	Property development in Hong Kong, Shenzhen, Guangzhou and Shanghai

China Overseas is the Hong Kong-based arm of the China State Construction Engineering Corp and has been established in Hong Kong since 1979. Buildings the group has erected dot the countryside of southern Guangdong and Hong Kong. China Overseas has progressively become involved with larger projects since 1985. In 1992 China Overseas Holdings listed its flagship firm bearing the same name. By 1993 the listed company acquired the construction operations of its parent, which now permit it to engage in the surveying, design and construction of a wide range of building and civil engineering projects, which include a contract for the main terminal of the new Hong Kong airport. It has carried out projects in 20 countries. In 1994, the listed company also acquired an 11.3% stake in a power plant in Shaoguan and a 50% stake in a cement plant in Shenzhen. The group, after having concentrated on property development in Hong Kong and Guangdong, is presently moving toward the development of additional properties in Shanghai.

CHINA RESOURCES (HOLDINGS)

Listed flagship:	China Resources Enterprise
Controlled since:	1992
Principal activities:	Property development and China industrials
Listed vehicle:	Ng Fung Hong
Listed since:	1995
Principal activities:	Pork and food distribution in Hong Kong
Listed vehicle:	China Resources Beijing Land
Listed since:	1996
Principal activities:	Beijing property development

China Resources was set up in Hong Kong in 1948 as China Resources Company to act as the general trade agency for China's trading needs. In 1983 the group was reorganised and renamed China Resources (Holdings). In 1992 it acquired a back-door listing, which was renamed China Resources Enterprise. From the perspective of the listed company, China Resources is very much a property developer with a few industrial and food-related investments, but at the holding company level, China Resources is an active investor in all facets of Hong Kong's economy and engages in department store operation, food distribution, shipping, and infrastructure and equity investments.

It reports directly to the Ministry of Foreign Trade and Economic Cooperation (MOFTEC), China's version of Japan's industrial policy formulation ministry, the Ministry of Trade and Industry (MITI). It was formerly known as the Ministry of Foreign Relations and Trade (MOFERT). China Resources is thus seen as a state-owned corporation under ministerial guidance. It operates an estimated 200 subsidiaries worldwide, with businesses ranging from commodities trading, to property development and banking. But the core business has remained its role as an importer of Chinese goods into Hong Kong as well as an exporter of key equipment into China.

The listed flagship

China Resources Enterprise (CRE) is the 51% listed vehicle of China Resources Holdings. CRE was formed through a back-door listing in September 1992, in which the company issued 276mn new shares at HK$3 each. In the early 1990s, CRE faced difficulties in developing an autonomous investment strategy, with final decisions hailing from Beijing. In 1995, however, renewed indications that Hong Kong management had secured new projects from CRH with MOFTEC's blessing sparked off new interest in the stock. The company strengthened its recurring income base in late 1993 through the acquisition of a 55% stake in Shenyang Brewery. However, it resold half its stake to South African Breweries for Rmb125–150mn one year later. The stake, in this case, fits in with a long term strategy to develop China's beer market with a strong foreign partner. Operations of the listed company remain heavily reliant on property income, though the company has been at pains to diversify into other investments. Property is expected to be a driver of profit growth, particularly after the massive 2.2mn sq feet

Tsing Yi redevelopment project takes shape after 1997. CRE holds a 55% stake in the project.

Other listed companies

The parent decided in 1995 to list on the Hong Kong stock exchange and at the same time inject a 26% stake in pork distributor, Ng Fung Hong. In November 1996, the listed company completed a spin-off on the Hong Kong stock exchange of a Beijing property company, China Resources Beijing Land, acquired in 1994.

CHINA TRAVEL SERVICE (HOLDINGS) HK LTD

Listed vehicle:	China Travel International Investment
Listed since:	1992
Principal activities:	Shenzhen theme park operation, hotel operation, freight forwarding

China Travel was founded in 1927 and now operates under the State Council. The Hong Kong subsidiary was founded in 1985 and has since invested in hotels, tourist parks, travel agencies, property and air and freight services. The Hong Kong company also listed its own subsidiary in Hong Kong in 1992, with the businesses under operation having been injected by the Hong Kong parent. The company had kept a relatively low profile, and had by the mid-1990s developed a reputation among some investors for being a less than well-managed group. The group is believed to have turned a corner in the fall of 1995, when younger managers joined management.

China Travel's hallmark is travel agencies, as tourists transiting Hong Kong on their way to China have learned. For travellers experiencing mix-ups during their travels in China, China Travel tends to be associated with the grief experienced negotiating one mode of transport (pre-arranged tours excluded). China Travel is also responsible for issuing travel visas to China and has acted as sole agent for the Kowloon to Guangzhou train. The company's staff has grown to about 15,000 in Hong Kong.

During the mid-1980s, China Travel received the go-ahead by the State Council to build and operate a series of theme parks in Shenzhen. The parks have proved popular with mainland tourists, putting Shenzhen on the map as an in-country tourist destination. The parks have also been injected into the listed company. With the arrival of younger managers at the listed company, additional investments have been planned. One departure was in mid-1996 when the Hong Kong parent injected a stake in a power station from western China into the listed company. Many analysts and investors were left wondering what the synergies between travel- and transport-related investments and power stations were. The rationale given by the group was that the group was seeking profitable investments, and with returns on investment likely to be over 20%, the investment in a power station was good for shareholders. In September 1996, the company was back on track with a HK$910mn acquisition of the three-star Metropole Hotel in Kowloon from its parent. The company has also been looking to expand its cooperation with its parent in running hotels in the mainland, as well continuing to search for new infrastructure investments.

GUANGDONG ENTERPRISES (HOLDINGS) LTD	
Listed flagship:	Guangdong Investment
Controlled since:	1987
Principal activities:	Diversified conglomerate investing in Hong Kong and Guangdong
Listed vehicle:	Guangnan Holdings
Listed since:	1994
Principal activities:	Food distribution in Hong Kong and China, supermarket operation

Guangdong Enterprises is Guangdong's leading holding company, with stakes in key enterprises throughout the province and other parts of China, and total assets of some US$1.6bn at the end of 1995. Guangdong Enterprises' investments are spread out among trading, manufacturing, infrastructure, property, hotels and finance. In 1993, the greatest contributions came from property (41.56%) and manufacturing (25.0%). During 1995 and 1994, the major source of operating income came from trading and property operations. In 1995, trading contributed 55.9% of operating profit before exceptionals, and property contributed 22.1% of operating profits before exceptionals.

Guangdong Enterprises raises capital where it can for companies under its tutelage. In February 1994, Guangdong Enterprises was responsible for the listing on the London Stock Exchange of the US$100mn Guangdong Development Fund. But its cost of funding can also be quite high. In June 1994, for instance, Guangdong Enterprises issued US$150mn in floating rate notes (FRNs) due 1999 at six-month LIBOR plus 200 basis points. The principal reason for this relatively high cost of capital is high leverage, nearly eight times that of its listed flagship, Guangdong Investment. Guangdong Enterprises can handle such high debt levels given its status as a sovereign borrower.

A number of injections of companies from Guangdong Enterprises and/or from the Guangdong provincial government into Guangdong Investment remain to be carried out over the coming years. A number of transactions engaged in by itself and its two listed companies are related-party injections. We will go into further detail in Chapter 7.

GUANGDONG INTERNATIONAL TRUST AND INVESTMENT CORP (GITIC)

Listed flagship:	GITIC Enterprises Ltd.
Listed since:	1997
Principal activities:	Marble, construction materials, property

Guangdong International Trust and Investment (GITIC) was first created in 1950 under the direct control of the Guangdong provincial government. In 1980 it was established as Guangdong province's principal funding vehicle in international markets. It operates 23 wholly-owned subsidiaries and 12 additional majority controlled subsidiaries. In 1993, consolidated assets stood at Rmb13 bn. In theory, it shares many of the investment aims of CITIC Beijing, except that its reach is regional rather than national. In practice, as an investor, it also shares some of the same investments and projects as Guangdong Enterprises. Some of the issues discussed below are very much intertwined with issues we will discuss in our presentation on Guangdong Enterprises. At issue are long term issues regarding Guangdong province's economic fundamentals. The company was rumoured in 1993 to be close to acquiring a back-door entry onto the Hong Kong stock exchange, but at the last minute was advised by authorities that it would be unwise for it do so. The back-door entry was cancelled. In mid-1996, press reports indicated that GITIC would seek a listing within the year, but a proposed listing was reportedly turned down by the Hong Kong stock exchange because the company lacked focus.

In March 1997, GITIC finally broke through Chinese government opposition to its listing when it listed its marble and granite products division in Hong Kong (despite a last minute controversy over official approval).

GITIC is organised along seven main business lines, including:

- Financial services
- Securities business
- Equity investments
- Real estate development
- Trading
- Leasing
- International operations

While CITIC answers to the State Council, GITIC answers to Guangdong Province. In the best of all worlds, it is considered to be part of the government of Guangdong province and to be fully backed by the province's government. At the same time, until 1993, government backed entities received similar treatment in international debt markets and typically received ratings equal to that of the state government. In 1994 and 1995, organisations such as GITIC all came up for credit rating reviews. While Moody's China sovereign rating remained at A3, GITIC, by mid-1995 had been downgraded to Baa2.

In addition, to the changing relationship between Beijing and Guangdong province, in which Guangdong has seen the funds it receives from Beijing reduced, GITIC has taken on a number of large projects, including the task of financing many of Guangdong's new superhighways (that of Hopewell Holdings in the early 1990s being the most well known). As a result, debt and contingent liabilities had by 1992 and 1993 soared to new heights. Total debt of Rmb10.2bn at the end of 1993 translated into a total debt to equity ratio of 6.14x, while at the same time guarantees extended by the group represented an additional Rmb7.9bn of contingent liabilities (amounts which GITIC would be called upon to honour in the case of default by the parties being guaranteed).

Equity as a percent of assets stood at 12.7% at the end of 1993 (1989: 6.7%), which was considered by Moody's in a June 1995 report on GITIC as a strong measure of capital adequacy. Equity as a percent of loans, investments and guarantees stood at 9.1% in 1993 (1989: 6.4%). That this picture represented an improvement over the late 1980s was partly due to a capital injection of about US$100mn by Guangdong province in 1992.

The issue of downgrading in 1995 based on data presented in the 1993 balance sheet does not make sense from the point of view of fundamentals, as the picture reported in one of Moody's own reports on GITIC pointed to an improvement in the company's financial position. As discussed earlier, Moody's downgrades came as a result of Beijing turning down requests for guarantees. One might argue that Moody's was downgrading GITIC just when its financials were improving, as shown in the financial analysis of the profit and loss account and the balance sheet of GITIC to 1993. A number of profitability, liquidity and capital adequacy measures highlighted in Moody's June 1995 report, for instance, show the company's vitals as improving. Equity as a proportion of assets, between 1989 and 1993, improved from 6.7% to 12.7%. During the same period, return on average assets grew from 0.67% to 1.33%. However, were one to argue the issue of downgrade in corporate debt from a perspective that the risk profile of Guangdong province changed during the early- to mid-1990s, Moody's argument with respect to the GITIC downgrade makes more sense. What is certain is that the application of ratings on Chinese institutions and their corporate debt is still very much in its infancy.

NORTH CHINA INDUSTRIES (NORINCO)	
Listed vehicle:	China North Industries Direct Investment Fund (Singapore)
Listed since:	1994
Principal activities:	Operation of industrial investments in the PRC
Listed vehicle:	Jianshe Motorcycle (Shenzhen B share)
Listed since:	1995
Principal activities:	Manufacture of motorcycles, mostly below 90cc

The People's Liberation Army's company, China North Industries Co, was created in 1988 and operates under the State Council. It is responsible for the operation of some 300 state enterprises and JVs with total fixed assets over Rmb60bn and over 800,000 employees. Norinco operations concentrate on firearms, ammunition, electronics and industrial and automotive enterprises. Some of the larger businesses include a JV with Mercedes Benz to produce diesel engines in Inner Mongolia, a float glass line plant in Liaoning, and an optical glass plant in Chengdu. In mid-1996, US-based Chinese executives linked with the company were named by US officials during a sting operation against Chinese smugglers of AK-47 rifles into the US. Executives of Poly Technologies were also named.

An alternate structure for companies representing the interests of the Chinese army, or "PLA Inc" as financial journalist Tai Ming Cheung calls them, is to build a flow chart with the armed forces coordinating body, the Central Military Commission, at the head of the organisation. The next level of subdivision comprises individual military departments such as the PLA General Logisitics Department headed by General Wang Ke, and then down to army-backed companies such as China Xinxing and 999 Enterprise. Readers are referred to Tai Ming Cheung's July 1996 article on PLA Inc in *Institutional Investor.*

SHANGHAI INDUSTRIAL INVESTMENT (HOLDINGS)

Listed vehicle:	Shanghai Industrial Holdings
Listed since:	1996
Principal activities:	Tobacco, pharmaceuticals, cosmetics

The Shanghai Municipal Government, through its investment arm Shanghai Industrial Investment (Holdings) made its first venture into the Hong Kong equity market when it placed about US$120mn with investors in Hong Kong and overseas in May 1996. Unlike other red chips, the municipal authorities selected many of their investments for their listed vehicle directly from existing operations controlled by the Shanghai authorities, without necessarily injecting assets which had been previously owned by the group. Shanghai Industrial Holdings was only given its Hong Kong corporate identity in January 1996, a few months before the listing.

Only one Hong Kong business, Nanyang Tobacco, has had a long-standing relationship with Hong Kong. Another three major investments are industrial and cosmetics businesses from Shanghai. At the time of listing, the tobacco company was seen as the cash cow of the group, with the Double Happiness brand of cigarettes having established high name recognition as a luxury brand in China (but sold almost exclusively overseas and in duty-free shops). As the newest of the red chips to hit the market in 1996, investors took a strong liking to Shanghai Industrial. Expectations are that a number of high profile injections remain in the offing for 1997, with potential acquisitions including infrastructure projects and shopping centres in the Shanghai area.

SHOUGANG STEEL

Listed vehicle:	Shougang Concord International
Controlled since:	1993
Principal activities:	Steel production and trading, other investments
Listed vehicle:	Shougang Concord Grand
Controlled since:	1993
Principal activities:	Property
Listed vehicle:	Shougang Concord Century
Controlled since:	1993
Principal activities:	Non-ferrous metals trading
Listed vehicle:	Shougang Concord Technology
Controlled since:	1993
Principal activities:	Industrials, property

Shougang, or First Iron & Steel Corp, has attracted the most attention and negative publicity for a red chip, following a scandal that rocked the entire Beijing Municipal Government in early 1995, and which led to a number of arrests and early retirements for company executives. The story of Shougang's decline in 1994 and 1995 closely mirrored the failing health of senior leader Deng Xiaoping, as it had been seen as China's largest would-be sprawling conglomerate.

Shougang's roots began in 1918 as Longyan Ore Holdings. At the time its principal activities were iron ore extraction. It operated under state control between 1949 and 1977. By 1983, it had become one of the first industrial enterprises to institute the responsibility system.

YUE XIU ENTERPRISES

Listed vehicle:	Guangzhou Investment
Listed since:	1992
Principal activities:	Property development in Hong Kong and Guangzhou, Infrastructure
Listed vehicle:	Denway Investment
Listed since:	1993
Principal activities:	Auto production and distribution

The Yue Xiu group was incorporated in Hong Kong in 1985 as the Guangzhou Municipal Government's investment arm in Hong Kong. Its activities include import and export of Guangdong and PRC products, property investment and development and project management in Hong Kong, the PRC and Southeast Asia. Senior executives of Guangzhou Investment include Zhang Bohua, chairman of both the company and the Yue Xiu group, and Guo Peinan, vice chairman of the company and general manager of Yue Xiu. Many senior executives of the company served in the municipal government.

Denway Investment

The Yue Xiu Group holds a number of other strategic investments in the Guangzhou area, including steel mills, power plants and auto assembly plants. One of its higher-profile investments has been a stake in Guangzhou Peugeot and additional auto assembly and distribution companies. In 1992, the group and the Guangzhou Municipal government bundled their stakes in Guangzhou Peugeot with other automotive investments and listed them on the Hong Kong Stock Exchange in February 1993 as Denway Investment, in the process surprising a number of other investors in the Peugeot JV, including Peugeot itself. Yue Xiu's stake before listing was 26.3% before listing and 17.7% after listing.

Relations between the French management and its Guangzhou host were known to be poor, but after the Denway listing a new phase in uncordial relations was initiated. What had begun as a profit-making auto assembly operation in the mid-1980s deteriorated rapidly under China's austerity of the mid-1990s. The listed company in 1994 became the first recently listed red chip to register a loss, turning in a loss of HK$148.6mn (1993: HK$262.7mn profit).

Guangzhou Investment

In December 1992, the group listed its Hong Kong property portfolio and laid down investment aims for the listed company, Guangzhou Investment, which included a pledge that all Hong Kong property investments managed by the group would be channelled through the listed company. Guangzhou Investment, however, diverged from its original direction and invested in Guangzhou area infrastructure and industrial projects. One of its largest acquisitions was a 51% stake in one of China's leading cement plants, Zhujiang Cement, for US$51mn in May 1993. As part of the acquisition, Guangzhou Investment agreed to take over loans that were being held by Guangzhou International Trust & Investment Corporation. The net result of the transaction was to transfer the asset and debt associated with it from a Guangzhou financial institution to a listed vehicle of the Guangzhou government. Foreign investors received a stake in a prize cement plant, and Guangzhou authorities got to reduce their debt exposure.

Following additional acquisitions, which included a 51% stake for US$30mn in Guangzhou Paper Mill and additional stakes in Guangzhou area cement plants, Guangzhou Investment's share price soared in late 1993. However, beginning in late 1994 and throughout most of 1995, the company returned to a property investment strategy which stretched from Singapore to Guangzhou. Investors had second thoughts and left the share price to flounder. The picture worsened when it also became apparent that the company had bought into the cement and paper operations at the top of their earnings cycle and that earnings growth would only recover after China's and Guangzhou's economy had returned to a growth phase. In order to repair its image with investors, Guangzhou Investment in early 1996 began to renew talk of infrastructure investments, and by mid-1996 had acquired new stakes in Guangdong toll roads. The company restructured its toll road investments and was ready for independent listing on the Hong Kong stock exchange, which it achieved in December 1996.

Appendix 2B: Red Chips

Table 2.1: Partial list of Red Chips listed in Hong Kong

Listed company *(As at May 1, 1997)*	Market cap. (US$mn)	Main investments	Controlling group	Listing type	Origin	Year
China Aerospace	473.0	appliances; autos	China Aerospace	Back door	Beijing	1992
China Everbright Int'l	326.3	property; industrials.	Everbright	Back door	Beijing	1993
China Everbright Tech	113.7	appliance manuf.	Everbright	Back door	Beijing	1993
China Everbright-IHD	841.3	retail; property	Everbright	Back door	Beijing	1993
China Foods	130.8	food	CEROIL Food	Back door	Beijing	1993
China Overseas	2,692.4	property	State Construction Min.	IPO	Beijing	1992
China Merchants	953.7	shipping; industr.	Communications Min.	IPO	Beijing	1992
CNPC (HK)	754.6	oilfield production	China Nat'l Petr. Corp	Backdoor	Beijing	1993
China Pharmaceutical	130.4	vitamin C	Provincial govt.	IPO	Hebei	1994
China Resources	4,236.5	property; food	China Res Holdings	Back door	Beijing	1992
China Resources Beijing Land	845.5	office property	China Res Holdings	IPO	Beijing	1996
China Travel	1,578.9	theme parks	China Travel Serv.	IPO	Beijing	1992
CITIC Pacific	11,673.2	conglomerate	CITIC/CITIC HK	Back door	Beijing	1992
Continental Mariner	304.8	property	China Poly/CITIC	Back door	Beijing	1993
Denway Investment	256.1	automotive	Yue Xiu Enterprises	IPO	Guangdong	1993
Florens/COSCO Pacific	2,694.3	container leasing	COSCO	IPO	Beijing	1994
Founder (HK)	355.8	software development	Beijing University	IPO	Beijing	1995
Guangdong Investment	2,185.0	conglomerate	Guangdong Enterprises	Back door	Guangdong	1987
Guang Nan Hang	1,077.5	food distribution	Guangdong Enterprises	IPO	Guangdong	1994
Guangzhou Investment	1,346.7	property; infrastructure	Yue Xiu Enterprises	IPO	Guangdong	1992
GZI Transport	607.4	toll roads	Yue Xiu Enterprises	IPO	Guangdong	1996
Hualing Holdings	92.4	refrigerators; compr.	Yue Xiu Enterprises	IPO	Guangdong	1993

Appendix 2B: Red Chips

Table 2.1: Partial list of Red Chips listed in Hong Kong

Listed company *(As at May 1, 1997)*	Market cap. (US$mn)	Main investments	Controlling group	Listing type	Origin	Year
Ka Wah Bank	428.1	banking	CITIC Beijing	Investment	Beijing	1986
Min Xin Holdings	214.9	banking; insurance	Fujian govt; ICBC	Investment	Fujian	1987
Ng Fung Hong	1,495.6	food distribution	China Resources	IPO	Beijing	1995
ONFEM Holdings	207.6	property	CNNC	Back door	Beijing	1993
Oriental Metals	142.0	non-ferrous metals	CNNC	IPO	Beijing	1994
Poly Invst Holdings	128.9	industrials; property	China Poly/CITIC	Back door	Beijing	1993
Shanghai Industrial	3,900.0	tobacco; conglomerate	Shanghai govt	IPO	Shanghai	1996
Shougang Concord Grand	203.4	property; construction	Shougang	Back door	Beijing	1993
Shougang Concord Int'l	398.1	holding; metal trading	Shougang	Back door	Beijing	1993
Shougang Concord Century	49.3	non-ferrous metals	Shougang	Back door	Beijing	1993
Shougang Concord Tech	46.2	industrials; property	Shougang	Back door	Beijing	1993
Shum Yip Invst.	718.1	property; industry	Shenzhen govt	IPO	Shenzhen	1997
Shun Shing	478.1	property	COSCO	Back door	Beijing	1996
Simsen Metals	35.9	metals trading	CNNC Shenzhen	IPO	Guangdong	1994
Silver Grant	353.0	investment; metals	CNNC	Back door	Beijing	1993
Top Glory International	389.3	property	CEROIL Food	Back door	Beijing	1993
Wing Shan Int'l	64.6	power generation	NA	IPO	Guangdong	1993
TOTAL	**42,923.1**					

Sources: Company prospectuses, annual reports and other market data

CHAPTER 3

A quick look at three very different companies

Charles de Trenck

COSCO, Shougang and China Resources could not be more different from one another. China Ocean Shipping Co (COSCO) is the newest arrival among large state-backed companies. Its profit centres are focused and easily identifiable with China's growing export prowess. Shougang, having benefited from red-carpet treatment from its close association with Deng Xiaoping, is identified with the imperial aspect of China's industrialisation. China Resources is quite the opposite of COSCO and Shougang. It had always moved slowly, giving investors and banks the impression that it would let investments come to it without exertion. Recently, however, it has taken a more active role.

COSCO: The new kid on the block

COSCO is one of the latest groups to be created and is built around the growth in trade between China and the rest of the world. It answers to the Ministry of Communications, just as China Merchants does. Founded during the 1960s, its growth has been due to changes in the world shipping industry. Since the 1970s more and more goods have been shipped on container vessels. COSCO has been China's principal owner of such vessels and the exporter of about 50% of China's total containerised cargo. The group also holds interests in a number of ports in China.

COSCO's container fleet has grown by leaps and bounds. In late 1997 growth entered a new phase when the group put into operation six 5,250 twenty-foot equivalent unit (TEU) vessels. At the same time, because not one of China's ports (except Yantian, near Hong Kong) can accommodate these new Post-panamax vessels, and also because COSCO has its own designs on growth, the group has engaged in a reorganisation that will make Hong Kong its principal base of operations after 1997.

COSCO Pacific

Renamed as COSCO Pacific in 1996 (the company was listed in December 1994 as Florens Group), the listed subsidiary owns about 300,000 TEU in dry and refrigerated containers, putting it in the top five container leasing companies in the world. Its biggest client remains its parent, which leases about 90% of COSCO Pacific's capacity. In late 1995, the listed subsidiary also acquired from the parent a 50% stake in two berths at Container Terminal 8 (CT8) East. The terminal, operated by COSCO-HIT is one of Hong Kong's newest and handled about 1.2mn TEU in 1995 (about 10% of Hong Kong's total handling capacity in 1995) and 1.15mn TEU in 1996. The HK$2.6bn injection increased the listed company by one third, placing it among the top few listed red chips in terms of market capitalisation.

Building a case for making Hong Kong a base of operations

Though some details of COSCO's restructuring are still being released (in 1997–98), the big picture is built around 1) Hong Kong as a centre of COSCO operations, and 2) taking advantage of as many concessionary tax rates and cost reductions as possible. COSCO HK has argued its case to Beijing that the only way Hong Kong will remain competitive, particularly against Singapore's government-backed port operations, is to subsidise Hong Kong's terminal operations. The company recognises that China's leading ports will not be able to compete with Hong Kong for several years in terms of infrastructure, and that therefore subsidising Hong Kong's regional competitiveness is in China's best interest. At the same time, the group is building new terminals at main ports across China.

Container liner operations

Most operations are being managed out of Hong Kong, excepting the management of the group's 150 plus container vessels which are run from Beijing. COSCO's container vessels, which will witness the addition of several new 5,250 TEU vessels during 1996–98, are owned by COSCO Hong Kong and operated under long-term charter agreements from COSCO Beijing. Many COSCO vessels are foreign-flagged (a normal practice for most world-class carriers, but not necessarily for Chinese ship operators). COSCO has followed this arrangement in order to avoid China's import taxes as well as to reduce corporate taxes to the lowest level possible, as international shipping is highly competitive. These foreign-flagged COSCO ships are also permitted to make stopovers in Taiwan. Making the case for Hong Kong stronger is that the new 5,250 TEU vessels (nine on order, six of which to be delivered in 1996–97) are not expected to call at any China ports for several years to come — as no port is large or established enough. The Yantian port, one of China's only deep-harbour ports and situated right next to Hong Kong, is not considered a suitable candidate for establishing an entire base of operations until it has developed more fully.

Bulk vessel operations

COSCO's more than 200 dry-bulk carrying ships will potentially all be held under one division in Hong Kong. In late 1995, 113 vessels of 6mn dwt were managed out of Beijing. An additional 1mn dwt of tonnage is distributed among Xiamen, Singapore and Shenzhen. In February 1996, COSCO (HK) Shipping was launched in Hong Kong with nearly 100 vessels aggregating about 4.8mn dwt. Most of the vessels under the Hong Kong company are in the Panamax, Handymax and Handysize categories, with close to half the tonnage having been built in the 1990s.

Creative financing

COSCO has also earned a reputation as a cut-throat financier for its vessels. In the 1980s it relied on China's developing country status to win concessions from German shipyards, most notably Bremer Vulkan. More recently, it has commissioned the construction of the Empress class of container vessels in Taiwan through third-party arrangements. While doing so, it has been able to take advantage of the Taiwan government's generous support of its shipbuilding industry. In early 1996, Japanese finance houses, which typically support strategic Japanese shipbuilders, were said in the shipping press to have been offended by COSCO when it asked Japanese houses to finance a new batch of orders placed with Korean yards. Advantageous financing terms for new vessels, which can cost over US$80mn for each 5,250 TEU vessel, is often arranged by COSCO for vessels which are not directly owned by it. Instead, the vessels are held by third parties, as in the case with Taiwan-built vessels, and chartered back to COSCO on long-term bareboat charters. It remains to be seen, under the 1996 COSCO restructuring, which subsidiaries and associates will take on vessels operated under such arrangements.

In 1997, COSCO entered a new phase when it entered the Hong Kong market in a substantial way, tying up with the Lai Sun group.

SHOUGANG STEEL: A model state company rocked by controversy

Shougang, or the Capital Iron and Steel Company, is the prototypical story of *guanxi,* connections, gone sour. Zhou Guanwu, the Company's former chairman, led Shougang to become a sprawling steel conglomerate complete with its own Peruvian mine, its own fleet of bulk vessels and its own bank. That the Company became so powerful was due to Zhou Guanwu's special relationship with Deng Xiaoping, after Zhou served in the army under Deng's command in 1937. Using his connections, Zhou won Deng's support to make Shougang one of the first state enterprises to institute the responsibility system. Under the system, Shougang was bound to a formula whereby it agreed to pay 7% more each year in taxes regardless of profits (the arrangement was reported to have been cancelled as of the 1996 tax year). As a result it won wide powers to set its own targets. As Deng's health began to fail in 1994 concern grew that Shougang was headed for a fall. In 1995, these fears materialised with the forced retirement of Zhou Guanwu and the arrest of his son, Zhou Beifang, who headed Shougang operations in Hong Kong.

Vertical integration as holy grail

Shougang set out on a mission to find investments and assets in all corners of the globe to help it achieve the integration it dreamed of. Some of Shougang's more infamous investments included the

1992 purchase of Hierro Peru iron mine for US$312mn, at up to six times its estimated book value, and the acquisition of a Los Angeles steel rolling mill for US$400mn, which is now reported to be stored in Shandong warehouses.

Shougang even developed its own fleet to transport its iron ore from Peru to China, some of which have been injected into Shougang Concord International in Hong Kong. It also ventured into finance through the operation of its own bank, Huaxia Bank (see Chapter 4). Its guiding principle behind growth has been that of vertically integrating operations along lines inspired by Soviet planners.

Coming to Hong Kong

In 1992, Shougang initiated a series of back-door entries on the Hong Kong stock exchange, often with the assistance of Li Kashing's Cheung Kong Holdings and his JV investment bank with the Canadian Imperial Bank of Commerce, CEF Capital. The perception in 1992 and 1993 was that Shougang was descending in glory onto Hong Kong and that its businesses were set to flower. The first of the Hong Kong back-door entries came through Tung Wing Steel, a company that had previously been under the control of the Allied Group.

What goes up...

From a China politics perspective, what investors did not take into account during the Shougang buying spree of 1993 was that connections could pull down as well as lift up. In 1995 Beijing's political climate changed as Deng's health became frailer. A series of high-profile purges was carried out against members of the Beijing Municipal Government, leading to a number of arrests and a suicide by a vice-mayor.

When everything was over, the Beijing party boss, Chen Xitong, had been kicked out of the Communist Party and placed under arrest. Under separate actions, but nevertheless viewed as the first real clean-up in Beijing after the full rise to power of Jiang Zemin, Zhou Guanwu announced he was stepping down from the company he helped create and his son was placed under arrest during a Chinese New Year visit to Beijing. Following these events, Deng

Zhifang, Deng Xiaoping's youngest son, also stepped down from his duties as vice-chairman of Shougang Concord Grand. The younger Deng had built up something of a reputation as a regular on Hong Kong's night club circuit. After the dust had settled, in October 1996, Zhou Beifang was tried in Beijing's People's Intermediate Court. Zhou, along with 11 other people, was said by the Chinese news service (18 October 1996) to have been charged in "very large" cases of taking and offering bribes and of concealing illegal property. According to a 15 November 1996 report in the *South China Morning Post*, Zhou Beifang received a suspended death sentence after being convicted of accepting bribes totaling HK$9.28mn between July 1993 and April 1994 and of offering bribes totaling HK1.2mn to co-conspirators.

3.1: Politics and share price performance

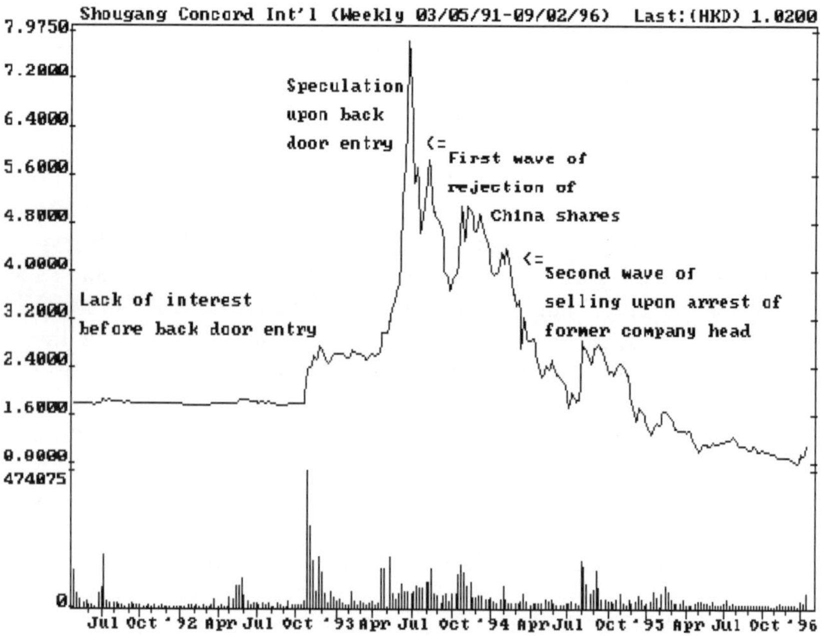

CHINA RESOURCES: The good corporate citizen

China Resources Holdings, the parent of listed subsidiary China Resources Enterprise, was, at the end of 1993 invested in a total of 347 projects totaling US$1.17bn. Some of the larger investments controlled by the group include:

- A 10% stake in HIT and its container handling facilities in Hong Kong (now injected into the listed company)
- New oil storage facilities on Tsing Yi island consisting of 20 oil tanks with 350,000 cubic metres storage capacity
- A 20% stake in the Shanghai-Nanjing Expressway
- Stakes in two 2x300 MW power stations in Hebei and Jiangsu provinces
- Participations in a number of high profile properties and hotels in Thailand, Beijing, Hong Kong and Macau
- Operation of a wharf and godown as well as bulk-shipping vessels in Hong Kong
- Operation of food trading companies, department stores, supermarkets and arts and crafts shops in Hong Kong

Among the major China-backed groups, China Resources gives the impression of being the squeaky clean one of the bunch. When it does something as small as buy a few million US dollar equity investment, it seeks a nod from Beijing. When Beijing came down on Jimmy Lai in 1995 for his *Next* magazine's criticism of Li Peng, China Resources divested itself of its shares in Giordano, a company that Lai had founded and that has arguably been a favourite investment of Western institutions. Mr Lai was already distancing himself from Giordano, but the message sent via China Resources, and through the licensing trouble a Beijing outlet of Giordano's was having, was that China enterprises had to make politically-correct investments. Jimmy Lai placed out his remaining 27% stake in February 1996, after the fall-out had ended.

Allowing investors to share in the fruits of a good investment

When China Resources Holdings and China Resources Enterprise acquire, inject or spin off operations, it is usually with the blessing of the State Council. Most other Beijing-backed companies also follow a similar policy. But China Resources sends the clearest message that it represents the interests of the state. In return, China

Resources has been able to obtain prize assets. In late 1994, it acquired an effective 29.6% stake in a Beijing property company, Beijing Huayuan, for US$44mn, or an estimated 3–4x earnings at that time. The earnings were unproven, but the acquisition price to earnings ratio was about as low as acquisitions will get for equity investors — far lower than what Hong Kong investors were accustomed to through companies such as CITIC Pacific and Guangdong Investment.

In the space of two years, this investment was groomed for a separate listing on the Hong Kong stock exchange. By late 1996, the Beijing property company had been re-packaged as China Resources Beijing Land and was listed in early November at about 10x its forecast earnings. Investors in China Resources were thus able to benefit from an upward re-rating of the original investment while the investment was held by the listed company. The two-year listing process represented one of the few instances where investors of a high-profile listed Chinese company were able to benefit from start to finish in the process of revaluing an asset for listing. With most companies, the revaluation of an inexpensive asset is typically done before the injection process begins.

On the other hand, China Resources has been known to drag its feet in completing deals, a trait that has from time to time unsettled investors. When it acquires, sells or spins-off, it usually gives investors one to two years advance notice. The long advance period is both a reflection of its own delays in obtaining necessary approvals and in preparing assets for listing. Another delay the listed company faces is tough scrutiny from the Hong Kong stock exchange, which often considers China Resources transactions as related-party transactions, and which therefore calls for additional verification of arm's-length negotiations between the parties. But the process is also a case of good corporate disclosure. At the end of the day, no investor is in the dark as to what the company's plans are.

Listing Ng Fung Hong

China Resources has also been taking lessons in structuring listings from those who have taught companies such as Guangdong Investment how to make money from the parent's assets. During the November 1995 listing in Hong Kong of the parent's food trading subsidiary, Ng Fung Hong, some similarities were to be observed with the injection of Guangnan (Holdings) Ltd by Guangdong Investment in November 1994. However, there are notable differences. China Resources Enterprise maintained its 26% stake as an associate; Guangdong Investment consolidated an effective 26% stake as a subsidiary through a complex holding company structure. The listing of Guangnan Holdings is discussed in detail in Chapter 7 on Guangdong Enterprises.

CHAPTER 4

Financing Chinese conglomerates — the banking system

Christian A Katz

Lenin's famous words that "in order to destroy the capitalist bourgeoisie one has to destroy their monetary system" is a fundamental growth criterion in its reverse form: The path to a socialist market economy, as envisaged in the Chinese economic reform process, has required the establishment of a new, efficient system to deploy and allocate financial resources. A single "monobank" institution such as the People's Bank of China (PBOC) of the pre-reform area, which acted as a money-issuing central bank and the sole commercial lending institution in China, may have been a sensible institution in the former central-plan economy. It could not possibly survive in an economy where individuals, alongside a central planning authority, would start to make their own investment and financing decisions. The reform era initiated by Deng Xiaoping in 1978 clearly called for a break-up of this administrative behemoth and the inauguration of other financial institutions that could handle a more decentralised allocation of the country's financial resources.

Today, in the late 1990s, it appears that China has a full set of financial institutions in place to run a modern growth economy (see appendix 4A for a description of some of China's most prominent banks). Unthinkable only two decades ago, we find two major stock exchanges — once the evil symbols of capitalism — in Shenzhen and Shanghai, where investors can mainly trade shares of state-owned and collectively-owned enterprises (SOEs and COEs), but also those of some private enterprises. There is an ever-growing primary bond market, in which the government and state-owned enterprises sell Rmb-denominated interest rate securities to Chinese investors, coupled to a slowly growing secondary market for actively traded bonds. The capitalisation of both equity and bond markets each surpassed the level of 10% of GDP in China as early as in 1993. Financial funds are also channelled from savers to firms through various banking institutions. Four state-owned, specialised commercial banks (Industrial and Commercial Bank of China, China Construction Bank, Agricultural Bank of China and Bank of China) constitute the backbone of the retail banking market. The central government has total control over three additional policy banks, namely the State Development Bank, the China Exim Bank and the Agricultural Development Bank, which are its prolonged arms to channel funds to state-owned units. Several smaller banks held by central or lower government units concentrate on servicing particular regions such as Guangdong Province or Pudong (next to Shanghai) and specific economic sectors, for instance trade and transportation. In 1996, China even saw the birth of the first and still only Chinese private bank since 1949, the Minsheng Bank, with the blessing of the central authorities. It was founded by 79-year old Jing Shuping, a true "capitalist" from the pre-communist era who had remained in China throughout the Cultural Revolution, with an initial capital of around US$170mn, about 85% of which originated from private businesses. Insurance companies, particularly the People's Insurance Company of China with a market share of over 90%, are also increasingly active. Foreign banks are slowly forcing their way into the local currency market, and there are a number of financial corporations in the securities and direct investment business.

The core of this new money-circulation scheme in China, however, is the domestic banking system as it has evolved since the start of financial reform. In terms of outstanding domestic bank loans alone the Chinese banking system has grown from Rmb0.19bn in 1978 to over Rmb5,000bn at the end of 1995. This represents an average growth rate of over 80% p.a., which even dwarfs the spectacular growth of China's real GDP over the same period. The advancement of China's leading companies such as CITIC, COSCO or China Merchants has not been independent from the development of the banking system. Investment needs financing, and the fight for profitable investments is as fierce as the contest for financial funds. To understand the rise of certain successful Chinese corporates therefore also means to understand the way in which these firms have been able to raise the necessary funds for expansion in the financial system. The present chapter tackles this question in two steps. First, we take a closer look at the stages of development which the Chinese banking system and the related financial markets have gone through. Second, we examine the characteristics of bank-industry relationships in China by comparing them to the ones we encounter in modern financial markets.

The emergence of a Chinese banking system

The Chinese government had no easy task when it decided to establish a comprehensive banking system in the mid-1980s. Several steps were required: The PBOC as the central bank had to be deprived of its commercial banking activities, which occurred in 1984. Domestic bond and stock markets, which were non-existent in the China of Mao Zedong, also had to be set up from scratch. Then again, the standard financial corporations — securities brokers, investment funds and so forth — that would act besides the banks as intermediaries between securities issuing institutions and investors had to be put in place too. In the 1980s all this took place under the strict guidance of China's central and regional governments, but still the legal and commercial framework for effective competition did not exist. This gap has slowly been filled in recent years. Respective cornerstones are new laws such as the Bankruptcy Law, the Financial Guarantees Law and the Commercial Bank Law, which started to be implemented only in the middle of the 1990s.

The state-governed development of a two-tier banking system

China's central bank, the PBOC, was until 1983 the single institution with the combined responsibilities of granting credit, issuing cash and monitoring the proper use of financial funds according to government planning. On January 1, 1984, this Soviet-style monobank was split in two. The PBOC was to continue its role as the actual central bank and a new bank, the Industrial and Commercial Bank of China (ICBC), took over its commercial lending activities. This left the central bank with a huge branch network, which today still spreads all over the country. It also created a new commercial banking giant overnight, since the ICBC inherited almost the entire loan portfolio of the PBOC. The government simultaneously decided to recreate the formerly abolished Agricultural Bank of China (ABC) and the People's Construction Bank of China (now the China Construction Bank, CCB). These two banks received the central responsibility of conducting the country's commercial lending business in the agricultural sector, and the capital and construction area respectively. They were complemented by the Bank of China (BOC), which had conducted all foreign-exchange transactions and international payments throughout the communist era. The BOC became independent from the central bank in 1979 and strengthened its role as the main state bank to conduct international financial transactions. Together, these first four commercial banks are still known as the "Big Four". As wholly state-owned specialised commercial banks they enjoyed a virtual monopoly position until 1995 in their respective banking sectors.

This is not to say that the Chinese government did not allow for the creation of supplementary banking institutions. Around a dozen commercial banks were established in the ten years following the break-up of the central bank. Some of them, such as Shenzhen Development Bank and Shanghai Pudong Development Bank, were set up by lower-level regional authorities to foster the development of specific regions, particularly in the Special Economic Zones. Others, such as the Bank of Communications (BOCOM) and the China Investment Bank, were set up by the central government with a specific sectoral development purpose. In the case of BOCOM this specific mission was to finance regional transportation links, which was a reason to concede some control over the bank from the state to regional governments; the China Investment Bank took on the role of managing loans and grants from supranational bodies such as the World Bank and the Asian Development Bank, before it ventured into broader commercial lending and was made a subsidiary of CCB in 1994. A third category of commercial banks was of those set up by state-owned conglomerates for their internal financing needs. Examples are CITIC Industrial Bank and China Merchants Bank, which have become familiar names in connection with their prominent parent companies. All of these commercial banks have been ultimately owned by the central state or lower level regional authorities. They were designed and tolerated for certain niche financing, but not as direct competitors to the Big Four.

The well-known trust and investment corporations (TICs) also came into existence in the 1980s. They quickly converted from direct investment vehicles owned by government entities or corporates and banks to very diverse money-lending institutions. As quasi-banks with a loosely defined business scope, the trust and investment corporations profited from a lack of financial regulation in the China of the early reform years. Until very recently they virtually acted like universal banks, except for two features: They were not allowed to collect demand deposits, and they could not establish a branch network. However, their internationally active members (ITICs), including the CITIC flagship, have been allowed to borrow abroad and channel foreign direct investments into the country. Another category of peripheral banking institutions consists of the Rural and Urban Credit Cooperatives (RCCs and UCCs). The more than forty years old RCCs, in which peasants had a collective ownership, are small-scale financial cooperatives which turned local savings into farm loans. After a vivid expansion in the 1980s, there were over 60,000 of these units temporarily or permanently employing some 500,000 people by the mid-1990s, but their loan market share has usually not exceeded 10% of the national total. UCCs were only established in the early 1980s. Usually controlled by government entities, corporates or banks, these savings vehicles have mushroomed to over 4,000 units of a comparatively small size by 1995. Today, many of these cash-abundant UCCs are merging into stand-alone commercial banks as witnessed, for instance, by the creation of the Beijing City United Bank and the Shanghai City United Bank.

Foreign banks, traditionally banned from conducting Rmb business in China, have strongly increased their local presence in the 1990s. Banks from Japan, the United States, Hong Kong, the United Kingdom and France have established the highest number of outlets. By the mid-1990s, foreign banks from over 30 countries held over 300 representative offices, more than 100 branches, around a dozen subsidiaries and half a dozen Sino-foreign joint ventures in China (see the development of foreign banks in appendix 4B). All these outlets are confined to certain open cities, which embrace all the major economic hubs of China, including Shanghai, Beijing, Guangzhou, Shenzhen, Dalian and Tianjin. Since foreign banks are restricted to foreign currency transactions, they have for long focused on servicing foreign-invested enterprises and expatriates within China. The pressure exerted by these banks on the Chinese government to liberalise access to the Rmb markets and Chinese clients has yielded slow progress. Only in the run-up to China's adoption of currency convertibility on the current account during 1996, foreign banks in Shanghai, Shenzhen, Dalian, and Jiangsu province were allowed to deal Rmb against foreign currencies in the spot market and access the Rmb interbank market on an experimental basis. A further hesitant step towards the broadening of foreign bank access to the domestic markets occurred when Beijing announced that a few banks would be allowed to conduct restricted Rmb business in Shanghai's Pudong development zone in 1997. The first batch of banks with a fairly limited licence to take Rmb deposits and conduct Rmb lending are HongkongBank (part of Hongkong and Shanghai Banking Corporation), Citibank, Bank of Tokyo-Mitsubishi and Industrial Bank of Japan. Even after the next batch of foreign banks allowed to conduct Rmb transactions, the Standard Chartered Bank, Dai-Ichi Kangyo Bank, Sanwa Bank and Shanghai-Paris International Bank (the first Shanghai joint-venture bank), was named in January 1997, there was no sign of real competition arising for Chinese commercial banks yet.

The structure of this early two-tier banking system has cast a long shadow up to the present day. Taken together, the Big Four still account for some 60–70% of the current domestic loan market. The BOC controls some 70% of the foreign exchange market today and holds around a quarter of its assets of about US$240bn in overseas markets. The CCB with assets of US$207bn in 1995 has emerged as a major borrower of international funds for infrastructure development in China with a total of over US$3bn in loans and bonds raised abroad up to end-1995. Profiting from its inheritance from the PBOC, the ICBC remained the largest bank in the country with a balance sheet in excess of US$370bn at end-1995.

It now runs a network of over 31,000 branches and offices with a staff of more than 550,000 controlling most of the Chinese retail banking market. In the rural areas it shares the retail sector with the ABC, which effectively controls the RCCs as quasi-subsidiaries and boasted assets of almost US$150bn at the end of 1995.

Why have the smaller commercial banks and the non-bank financial institutions in China not captured a higher share of the domestic financial markets? The core of the answer is central planning. How could the government let market competition decide on the distribution of financial resources, when it intended to continue central planning for the largely unprofitable state-run sector of the transitional economy? The economic logic of transition in China has so far been to run a market-oriented sector (private and collective enterprises) parallel to the state-run sector (state-owned enterprises under the central plan). This meant that the central government had to strike a deal with the financial corporations. Some activity in the informal financial sector, dominated by the TICs and the credit cooperatives, could be accepted — the majority of the banking system had to remain under government control. And there is no mistaking this: "control" is the most often heard expression used by officials from the PBOC when it comes to describing the process of financial reform in China.

The means of central control over the banking sector were manifold and have only softened very recently. The domestic credit plan, which governed the amount of credit to be granted by each bank, and the prescription of interest rates on Rmb assets were the strongest direct monetary control tools used by the central bank. In external relations, the State Administration of Foreign Exchange (SAFE) controlled the amount and type of foreign currency that banks or any other firms could raise. So, the kind of growth that made the four major Chinese banks become the world's 10th (ICBC), 31st (BOC), 38th (CCB) and 54th (ABC) largest banks in terms of assets by mid-1996 as reported in *The Banker* (1996) was a dictated growth. The four banks had their assigned loan customers in the respective sectors, they enjoyed preferential access to central bank funding and they were not constrained by profitability considerations in their activities. Competition between banks and non-banking financial institutions mainly occurred on the funding side. The name of the game was "how to capture the Chinese savings pool in deposits" — an attractive challenge in a country with an average 38% savings/GDP ratio in the years 1984–94. In the presence of prescribed deposit rates, bank branch extensions, marketing and rerouting of loans granted to SOE clients were seen as the crucial tools to divert cash holdings into bank deposits. Again, none of the institutions were better equipped with the initial financial resources to succeed through such measures than the Big Four, in particular the ICBC.

The challenge of transition: attempts at decentralisation

Domestic enterprise bond and equity markets, established in 1986 and 1989 respectively, have somewhat alleviated the burden of Chinese corporates to seek outsider Rmb capital from state-controlled banks only. In theory, this was a turning point — Chinese corporates have from then onwards been able to consider an entire three-fold range of financing sources (see also appendix 4C):

First, there are the loan funds extended, or "directly intermediated", by domestic banks and quasi-banks. The process of raising loan funds has, however, not been straightforward. State-owned enterprises (SOEs) can usually turn to the state-owned, specialised commercial banks for extensive funding. These banks have until the end of 1996 had credit lines centrally allocated and enforced on them, coupled with informal or formal political pressure to extend funds to specific SOEs. Even as late as 1994/5, SOEs still accounted for 70–80% of borrowing from state-owned commercial banks. Other firms, i.e. collectively-owned enterprises or private Chinese and foreign-invested firms, have not been included in the central production and credit plans of the State Planning Commission (SPC), and have therefore often turned to alternative lenders. These include the other commercial banks (subject only to a "broader credit plan" with less stringent enforcement), the trust and investment corporations, credit cooperatives and finance companies. Most of these institutions, such as regional TICs, have made the availability of credit dependent on political pressure exercised by the borrowers, personal or some sort of "innovative financing" — ingenious ways of breaching official lending limitations or loan interest rate regulations — to satisfy the growing demand of their customers. One example quoted by foreign joint-venture managers in China is that their enterprise is allowed a three-year Rmb credit line for fixed assets investments by a non-bank financial institution for a certain amount, say Rmb50mn, but is only allowed to draw on half of this amount for real credit. All costs and fees are paid on the Rmb50mn line, which pushes the real all-in interest rate earned by the lender above the one prescribed by the central bank, in this case 10.98% p.a. (as of April 1997).

Second, many enterprises have been lured by the possibility of raising "indirectly intermediated" funds by issuing bonds or shares with the help of financial corporates (the intermediaries). However, the process is under tight control of national as well as regional authorities in China. In a complex web of regulatory-approval hurdles, companies wishing to issue Rmb-denominated corporate bonds or equities require at least a go-ahead from the SPC (which represents the State Council, China's central government), the local government of the province in which the company is located, as well as the State Commission for Restructuring the Economic System, and China's Securities Regulatory Commission. The PBOC also interferes in the issuing of bonds, since it sets the interest rate these securities may pay to investors. As a consequence, only SOEs have been allowed to issue corporate bonds, while the bulk of the bond market is represented by sovereign bonds and bonds issued by non-private financial institutions. In the domestic A share market, SOEs which only float a minority portion of their entire shareholding capital on the stock exchange have also dominated over COEs and private firms in terms of share issuance. But why has the government held such a tight grip on the securities markets? Among several reasons such as investor protection and issues of monetary policy, the most pressing has been to control the speed of privatisation in China. Not only do public shares transfer ownership to investors, but corporate bonds also transfer certain control rights to buyers, such as the right to take on the issuing firm's assets in case of repayment default. In China's gradual reform path, where the communist government still tries to "feel the stones under the feet before crossing the river", the transfer of corporate control rights from the state to the public through securities issues is necessarily a sensitive subject which prompts strict government control and supervision.

Third, Chinese corporates also have the opportunity of raising "direct-link" financing straight from investors without any interference from commercial or investment banking entities. The crucial direct investors are the central government in the case of SOEs, lower level governments in the case of COEs, and all those Chinese family entrepreneurs who put their savings into private enterprises with no more than seven employees. In the case of SOEs and COEs, the success of raising such finance is often the result of lobbying power. For those who run China's small-scale private enterprises, direct capital injections have to come from close family members and other *guanxi* investment circle friends. The restrictions for many smaller corporates to access the banking and securities markets have spurred the tendency to seek financing without intermediation from banks or other financial firms. This can prove to be a more efficient way of financing, but it requires that there are sufficient financial resources available outside the banking system. China's consistently high ratio of Currency in Circulation (= M_0) / GDP of more than 16% during the three years up to end-1994, by far exceeding the ratio of industrialised countries, or even a country like India, indicates that people continue to rely heavily on direct-link financing — in other words, the banking system still has a long way to go in order to efficiently circulate the non-cash financial funds according to the size of the economy.

In parallel to the widening of domestic financing sources, the Chinese government experimented with an increased participation of foreign financiers. Of the overseas "direct intermediaries", foreign commercial banks in particular were strongly encouraged in the middle of the 1980s and again after 1991 to lend to prime corporations in China. These borrowers were a set of centrally selected "window borrowers" comprising the Big Four, CITIC and a few other financial corporations (including the PBOC acting for the MoF). The foreign currency funds they could raise were normally on-lent to the actual producing enterprises in China, the SOE clients of the financial corporations. Chinese industrial corporates were only allowed to tap foreign banks on a case-by-case basis. In the years prior to 1992, the SAFE always kept the number of non-window borrowers below 50 per year. Only in 1994 and 1995, more than 100 non-financial corporates from China (including foreign-invested enterprises which did not require approval) borrowed foreign currency loans overseas. For many Chinese corporates this meant that they would seek foreign resources from the World Bank, foreign governments or other official creditors; however, these loans were also administrated by the Chinese central government, which favoured SOEs and Sino-foreign joint ventures with an SOE partner over other firms.

Access to the international bond markets also remained restricted to the financial "window borrowers". Of these, the BOC, CITIC and the PBOC alone accounted for 66% of the US$14.3bn raised in overseas bond markets between 1984 and 1995. Industrial corporates had to lobby for some of the foreign currency funds borrowed by these financial corporations, or they could try to issue equity to foreigners. The latter was highly difficult, since issuing shares to foreigners was a type of privatisation that fostered non-Chinese control over Chinese enterprises — which has never been a central government priority! Accordingly, only a select number of Chinese firms, mainly SOEs, were allowed to raise foreign currency funds through the official issuance of B, H, or N shares, with the blessing of the Chinese authorities. By the end of July 1995, 41% of the B-share market capitalisation of US$2.4bn (Shanghai and Shenzhen) was represented by SOEs, 39% by Sino-foreign joint ventures and only 20% by COEs. Not a single Chinese private firm was listed there. The government was taking an even stricter stance when choosing firms for issues of N and H shares. After three years of such activity, at the end of July 1996, 89% of the H share market capitalisation of US$3.9bn was accounted for by 19 SOEs, with one joint venture and one COE making up only 9% and 2% respectively. Both N shares at that time, Shandong Power and Huaneng Power, were SOEs too. Chinese banks, bound to remain fully held by public entities, were not among the firms foreigners could hold shares in.

To become equity owners in Chinese firms, foreigners often had to take recourse to indirect holdings in shares, as represented by the "red chips" and discussed in other chapters of this book. Alternatively, they would conduct direct investments (FDI) in China. Driven by tax advantages, the establishment of the Special Economic Zones, the liberalisation of several coastal cities (including Shanghai) and other incentives, private foreign funds have tended to come preferably through the "direct-link" financing route in the form of FDI to China. Within relatively short time, China became the developing country with the highest contracted FDI inflows in the world, attracting US$37.7bn in 1995 and over US$40bn in 1996 alone. More than many China-observers seem to acknowledge, this is the result of the limitations foreigners have faced when trying to conduct portfolio investments in the country.

The consequence of this cautious financial system decentralisation has been a heavily biased use of financing channels in China. On the one hand, the Big Four have always accounted for the majority of all loans disbursed in China, holding several hundred US$billion in their portfolios by the mid-1990s. Until 1995, these banks were under the direct control of the central government and not free in the choice of their borrowers. Supported by the central credit plan, the prevention of Rmb interest rate competition and the tight allocation of securities issue quotas, the state has therefore been able to keep the majority of the banking system in the hands of these specialised commercial banks. On the other hand, loans from other institutions have grown fast but remained at a relatively low level, while the securities markets have not yet diminished the importance of direct investment. Total outstanding domestic loans of all UCCs, RCCs, TICs and finance companies only totalled US$120bn at the end of 1995, while outstanding Chinese bank loans stood at over US$480bn equivalent. The total raised in China through the issuance of Rmb-denominated equities and bonds ever since the inception of such activity has not come close to the loans managed at the level of the Chinese specialised commercial banks. Also in the raising of money from overseas sources, Chinese banks, corporates and government bodies have heavily relied on bank loans. Private lending has outpaced the flow of official credit, and foreign direct investment has dominated over funds raised in the securities markets (see appendix 4C).

Clearly, the old financing links between SOEs and the state-owned banks (constituting the bulk of the first financing mode) only softened very slowly. The government maintained control of financial flows, but at a high cost. Managers at Chinese banks were not in a position to turn down loan requests from SOEs, neither were they inclined to. They followed the regional and central government's growth objectives instead of self-devised profitability targets. Through their holdings in securities companies and TICs, the Chinese state-owned banks also had a strong influence in the securities markets. The BOC, ICBC, ABC and CCB used to act either through their parent entities or their subsidiaries as arrangers of securities issues and securities traders in the secondary markets. The incomplete legal framework and weak financial supervision fostered the manipulation of the securities markets by the Big Four — or more specifically by individuals with the backing of such powerful financial giants. Given the many financial scandals prior to the introduction of the Commercial Bank Law in 1995, it was clear that "Chinese walls" within banks were hardly existent or abused in the young banking culture in China.

After ten years of living with a slowly decentralising two-tier banking system, China was in 1994 still dominated by state-owned universal banks, which acted under the "soft budget constraints" of the central plan and nurtured the abuse of political power allowed by their monopolistic positions. The Chinese banks were therefore still virtual government agencies, not banks in the true sense.

The "commercialisation" of the Chinese banking system

The Chinese banks accumulated vast amounts of loans against loss-making SOEs up to the middle of the 1990s. This is hardly an astonishing fact. With the government clinging on to a centrally planned state sector, funding them at subsidised interest rates through dependent commercial banks, the fate of these banks has been contingent on how these SOEs are faring. In 1994/5, the Chinese banks still allocated 70–80% of their loans to SOEs, of which 40–45% were loss-making and half of the balance were breaking even and only about 30% were making a profit. As a consequence, the state-owned banks are estimated to have 20–40%

of their loan portfolios tied up in non-performing loans, i.e. loans for which interest payments and principal repayments are overdue for more than three consecutive three-month periods. Chinese bank officials usually put this ratio at 20%, but foreign market observers often estimate the bad debt ratio to be more in the region of 30–40%. Consider in the table below what this means for the Big Four alone, when one estimates in line with Nicholas Lardy, a leading China-scholar in the US, that one third of loans held by Chinese banks are non-performing:

Table 4.1: Comparison of China's four major banks
(as of end-1995, in US$mn[1], except for ROAA and staff)

	ABC	BOC Grp[2]	ICBC	CCB
Total capital funds	4,905	12,361	11,147	4.810
Total assets	148,003	272,453	373,614	207,116
Total commercial loans	82,982	138,962	178,072	93,515
Loan loss provisions	517	2,224	1,359	598
Net after-tax profit in 1995	233	873	561	742
ROAA[3] in 1995	0.15%	0.34%	0.16%	0.40%
Medium ROAA 1991–94	0.21%	0.63%	0.87%	0.25%
Staff	564,731	213,767	569,983	356,864

1. Rmb/US$ = 8.3174 at year-end 1995.
2. Includes the wholly-owned subsidiaries of the Bank of China, in particular the "sister banks" in Hong Kong.
3. Return on average assets, i.e. after-tax profit over average of total assets in current and previous years.

Sources: Figures and calculations based on the annual reports of the four banks.

After deduction of the negligible loan loss provisions made by these banks, the accumulated bad debt would equal US$162.9bn, several times the four banks' capital base. Following Nicholas Lardy's argument, even if the banks had immediately discontinued new loans to their defaulting borrowers in 1996 and finally recovered 50% of their non-performing loans from the proceeds of liquidating insolvent SOEs, the total financial losses would have amounted to US$81.5bn! This would be equivalent to 11.7% of China's GDP of US$694bn in 1995 and would even exceed the relative costs of the S&L banking crisis in the US (2% of GDP), the

1994/1995 banking crisis in Mexico (some 5.7–10% of GDP) and the recent asset-deflation banking crisis in Japan (4% of GDP).

The profitability record of the four major state-owned banks does not inspire confidence that these institutions can boost their capital base independently through retained earnings. The median return on average assets, ROAA, a meaningful profitability measure in the face of strongly growing assets and a low capital base, of the Big Four did not exceed the median ROAA of commercial banks in other Asian developing countries over the years 1991–94, such as the Philippines (2.44%), Thailand (1.35%), Malaysia (0.92%) or Korea (0.91%), as reported by Thomson BankWatch. The profitability record of the Chinese banks did not significantly improve in the financial year 1995 either, leaving it in the hands of the central government to tackle the looming systemic risk linked to the much needed SOE reform.

In 1994/5, the central government responded with a long-awaited reform measure: It created the three policy banks, the State Development Bank (SDB) for state-led capital construction and infrastructure financing, the China Exim Bank for state-governed trade financing, and the Agricultural Development Bank (ADB) for state-led agricultural development financing. These banks assumed all policy lending functions from the CBC/ICBC, the BOC and the ABC and officially alleviated these from government-dictated funding of SOEs. The government subsequently promulgated the first Commercial Bank Law and a new Central Bank Law in order to define the competitive position of all commercial lenders and reduce excessive political pressure in the banking system. The magic word was the "commercialisation" of the Chinese banks — what this meant was that commercial banks, including the Big Four, were now held to operate with responsibility for their own risks and free from interference by government units. Only the policy banks should now be used for sector-specific loans made in the interests of the central government, as they are, for instance, necessary for the construction of the immense Three Gorges hydropower plant (through the SDB), the importation of army material (through China Exim Bank) or the financing of state-run agricultural projects (through the ADB). All commercial banks, as opposed to the policy banks, lost their sectoral monopoly positions and were set to compete with each other. The three hitherto domestically oriented ABC, CCB and ICBC reacted swiftly by each opening their first branch in Hong Kong, where the Bank of China had already advanced to being the second largest bank, in the course of 1995. It all seemed to finally pull the trigger for the rise of a market-oriented, competitive banking system in China — or did it?

Two features of the reform steps taken by the government in the course of 1994/5 have to be noted. For one, the policy banks are not designed to take over the bad loans accumulated by Chinese banks prior to the middle of the 1990s. They are seen as new institutions that should start from a clean basis. Thus, commercial banks remain stuck with their non-performing loans and their long-time SOE clients. Instead of taking the bull by the horns, the government has placed a bet on the gradual, self-regulating power of the state-owned commercial banks. The second important feature of the government's commercialisation effort is the drift of the banking system towards a separation of commercial and investment banking equivalent to that applied in the US in the 1930s and in Japan after World War II. Through the Commercial Bank Law of 1995, all Chinese banks are now banned from the domestic securities business other than the trading of bonds. In a wave of divestments, the banks have sold off or liquidated the TICs, finance firms and securities subsidiaries that used to be under their control. The establishment of a Securities Law, Trust Investment Law and Fund Management Law is already under way. These laws will complement the regulation of commercial banking in China by setting the legal framework on the investment banking side, where mushrooming non-bank financial institutions have pursued their activities within a very loose legal environment. Taken together, the characteristics of this commercialised, if not yet highly competitive, banking system are set to partly redefine the linkages between banks and their industrial clients in China.

Bank-industry linkages in China

Which role model of bank-industry linkages to apply in China?
Chinese economic leaders tend to insist that they have pursued a reform path with "Chinese characteristics", meaning that the country's complex situation of banking and industrial sector ties has required solutions that cannot be simply copied from mature financial systems. However, the features of China's emerging financial framework can be compared to patterns of bank-industry linkages found in other markets. There are basically three role models that describe the fundamental relationship which banks can have versus their industrial clientele. In a "German model" of universal banking, banks can conduct a full range of commercial and investment banking transactions with their clients and take substantial equity stakes in industrial corporates. Banks can then exert a strong corporate governance function, as for instance demonstrated by Deutsche Bank's influence in German industrial firms such as Daimler Benz, through the equity holdings, loan exposures and board seats they hold in their corporate clients. In a capital market-based "Anglo-American model" of narrow banking, the securities markets replace the banks as those institutions which enforce financial discipline on industrial managers and effectively exert corporate control. The prime example of strong, but often informal, links between banks and their corporate clients is the "Japanese model" of conglomerate *keiretsu* structures.

As a result of the financial reform path outlined, the situation created in the Chinese banking system seems increasingly comparable to the bank-industry linkages found in Japan, much more so than to the structures encountered in Germany or the United States. After permitting the state-owned specialised banks to grow into universal banking mammoths for a decade, the Chinese authorities have rejected the basis of the German approach and implemented a separation of commercial and investment banking activities. Unlike the situation found in the United States, the domestic capital markets have not grown to a stage where shareholders can enforce financial discipline on corporate managers or bond investors can force firms into liquidation in order to ensure repayment of their claims. The cautious privatisation programme of the Chinese state has left majority control of most large firms with government entities; hence, there is no active take-over market for firms, nor is there any legal framework that guarantees the actual property rights of securities holders. Instead, there are several factors, similar to Japan, which link banks to their borrowers, not least the ties they often share with respect to their common government owners. There are also more and more Chinese conglomerates, as shown in the context of the firms described in this book, which resemble Japanese *keiretsu* or Korean *chaebol* groups.

The bank-industry glue: non-performing loans, moral hazard, informal government links

Chinese banks are not allowed to hold equity stakes in non-financial firms, which is sometimes raised as an argument to show that no Chinese conglomerate, such as CITIC or China Merchants, or Chinese industrial group with certain bank relations can be compared to a Japanese *keiretsu*, such as Mitsubishi or Sumitomo. The truth is that the bank-industry links in China, particularly outside the well-known state-owned groups, are relatively subtle. Industrial firms, particularly the SOEs derive the bulk of their financing from bank loans. Due to the poor performance of at least half of all SOEs over time, such loans are often not serviced and appear unrecoverable. For the banks, such non-performing loans become quasi-equity stakes: they are not fixed income instruments because the return on these loans depends on the economic performance of the borrower. In that regard, the borrowing firms, similar to Japanese industrial firms that are principally dependent on funding from the major *keiretsu* bank, are informally dependent on the goodwill of their bank(s) not to call the loans and continue rolling them over in times of financial distress. This dependency is underlined by the fact that until 1995, when competition between banks was introduced, most non-financial corporations from different sectors had only one monopoly bank or one sectoral bank relationship.

The glue that binds many industrial firms to particular banks also sticks well at the other end. Since the three policy banks did not take over the non-performing loans from the commercial banks, the latter have been largely stuck with these claims. The managers of these banks, in particular the Big Four, are now prone to "moral hazard" in their lending decisions. This moral hazard, hidden actions against the interests of the bank owners, arises because the bank managers had never envisaged carrying any liability for lending to unprofitable SOEs in the past, since they assumed the state would cover the losses incurred through these policy loans. Even though the government officially decided to discontinue policy lending through commercial banks to certain SOEs in 1994/5, the bank managers have since then been inclined to continue and increase lending to these "bad" clients. If they did not do so, the same SOEs that have received policy loans from them in the past might face severe liquidity problems and threaten their banks with default on future interest and principal repayment. The bank managers, therefore, increase their exposure to their long-standing good and bad clients. The government remains largely unable to detect this behaviour, because of its incomplete supervision capabilities, or to sanction the bank managers, because it has a direct interest in the survival of many bad SOEs and has only allowed very limited enforcement of bankruptcy procedures and asset liquidation on non-performing SOEs. So clearly, as within a traditional *keiretsu*, there is often an expectation of mutual support in periods of economic distress between banks and borrowers in China.

A further similarity to the bank-industry linkages in Japan is the widespread government influence, which in Japan is often accomplished through the Ministry of Finance or MITI. In China, government relationships that cement the ties between banks and borrowers are found at different levels. The government is the owner of all major commercial banks, all three policy banks, but also a wide net of industrial SOEs. That increases the dependence between the major banks and the major corporates, because their common owner will ultimately not let these units take independent actions such as the initiation of a major privatisation wave (triggered by SOEs), a major bankruptcy and liquidation wave (called on by banks) or a widespread freezing of credit lines (by the banks). The economic role and importance that banks have for their corporate clients is in this way much more pronounced than in financial markets such as the United States or the United Kingdom, where the government has no direct grip on the major commercial banks and industrial corporations. At the provincial or regional level, the government influence also often boils down to common ownership. A well-described example in this book is the case of the Guangdong provincial government, which controls such powerful business vehicles as Guangdong Enterprises, Guangdong ITIC and Guangdong Development Bank. Whenever Guangdong Enterprises or one of its many subsidiaries ventures into new projects, it is implicitly understood that the provincial ITIC or commercial bank provide financing, at least as the last solution if no other funding sources are available, and bridge any liquidity crises that may arise. Often this phenomenon also occurs in a market like Hong Kong, where the different bank and corporate units controlled by the same Chinese government entity establish branches, subsidiaries or affiliated companies that provide business for each other and support one another in their expansion plans.

An illustrative case of government influence that links banks and industrial corporates is found in the gigantic, state-led Three Gorges dam project. The construction of this hydropower plant, which will be the world's largest, has been assigned to the specially created state-owned China Yangtze Three Gorges Project Development Corporation. At the beginning of 1997, the total costs for this dam were estimated at around US$25bn. Most of the money required for the power equipment, the project management, etcetera, by the project company is being financed by the SDB, because of the high priority the central government has attached to this venture. There is no chance of the SDB or the project company taking any important decisions without government approval. This can also be expected to be the case in the linkage between other banks and all those firms, mainly SOEs, which carry out the actual massive construction works. When these firms have to fund the respective expansion of their operations in advance, and potentially without the SDB, because they are only indirectly responsible for the completion of the project, the central government as the owner of all major commercial banks such as the CCB, the ICBC or the BOC, will most certainly ensure that funding for these companies is available from the banks' side. Given the high prestige of the project, none of these firms, even if they are not directly state-owned, should have to worry about being forced into bankruptcy due to possible problems in the future.

Looking back to look ahead

Many corporates, particularly the many very small private businesses, will not necessarily be linked to their banks in the many ways described so far. However, the most significant features of Chinese bank-industry linkages have their mirror image in the Japan of the pre–Big Bang years. This might give us some understanding of the destination which the Chinese road of financial reform is leading to. In a Japanese model of informal cohesion between corporates and banks under the wings of different government entities, there arise various advantages. The government can more easily control the pace and regularity of growth, because it effectively controls both the real investment and the financing side of the crucial economic sectors. The model also provides for a certain resilience against minor cyclical reversals in the phase of fast economic development because banks tend not to abandon their borrowers at the first sight of looming financial distress. More importantly, the separation of the commercial and investment banking sides fosters a climate of narrow banking in which regulatory supervision within a weak legal framework is facilitated.

At the same time, the Japanese experience teaches us some less favourable lessons. Under such government-induced bank-industry marriages in the name of the national interest, corporates and banks strive for expansion and power — more the motives of politicians than managers. The focus of managers is clearly not on profits or shareholder value, which might undermine the worldwide competitiveness of these corporates and banks in the long run. Remembering that China's four major banks might have accumulated more than 11% of the country's GDP in worthless assets points out to what extent the Chinese banking system has been abused by the central government to support the growth of the economy. This leads to the next issue which is raised by the Japanese experience, namely that such an expansion can bring about immense systemic risks. Time-bombs such as the asset-inflation bubble in Japan are often ignored when governments shield corporate and bank managers from the burden of making arduous commercial choices on the basis of hard budget constraints. Unfortunately, while the build-up of a bubble such as the asset increase of the Chinese state-owned banks may be controlled by the government, the bursting of the bubble usually can not. The trigger is often pulled by a real shock such as a political conflict or a massive oil price rise.

Moreover, by the time the inherent fragility of such a banking sector arrangement becomes apparent, there suddenly arises strong pressure for deregulation. It is hardly pure historic coincidence that both Japan, after feeling the deep pain of a banking system crisis, as well as the United States, are abandoning the strict separation of the securities and commercial banking businesses. It could well be that the Chinese leadership views the move from a universal banking system to a government-controlled separated system in 1994–95 as a temporary move towards a different, more market-based environment. The current set-up of the banking system suggests that China is still in for a major financial system overhaul — be it the rise of more private banks, the introduction of foreign competition, or the deliberate boost of the domestic capital markets. Under the present arrangement, the looming risks have not been dealt with yet, and the state-owned banks can be complacent enough not to worry about their competitiveness. As long as this situation prevails, even corporate groups such as CITIC or Guangdong Enterprises, which do not suffer from specific funding problems with Chinese banks, will have strong incentives to tap foreign capital through the issuance of red chip shares and other financing vehicles.

Appendices

Appendix 4A: Selected Chinese bank profiles

BANK OF CHINA

The Bank of China is considered the country's most prestigious bank with, as its symbol, the Bank of China Tower reigning over Hong Kong's central business district. It is also China's oldest bank. Established in Shanghai in 1912, it managed to keep its door open through the 1949 Revolution and the Cultural Revolution in the 1960s as the specialised foreign exchange subsidiary of the PBOC. By the end of 1995, it operated 3,359 China branches and offices as well as 525 overseas branches and offices in cities such as Hong Kong, New York, London, Tokyo and Singapore. Many of these overseas outlets are held through wholly-owned subsidiaries and the 11 "sister banks" in Hong Kong (of which the largest are Sin Hua Bank, Kincheng Banking Corporation and Kwangtung Provincial Bank), which form part of the Bank of China Group. Hong Kong, where the BOC Group is the second largest banking institution behind the Hong Kong and Shanghai Banking Corporation and where it has advanced to one of the three note-issuing institutions, represents by far the most important international market for the bank. There it has not only advanced to become a strong retail market player with more than 17,000 employees and a 25% share in the territory's savings deposits, but it has also been the leading vehicle to channel financial resources from the territory to the mainland. Traditionally, around 50% of foreign direct investment in China comes from Hong Kong and is often transferred there through the BOC. In the period 1984–95, the BOC accounted for 24% of all Chinese borrowing in the international syndicated loan markets and for 26% of all Chinese overseas bond issues. At least 40% of its profits are believed to be currently generated overseas. Constantly expanding its business, the BOC established a stand-alone merchant banking group, Bank of China International Holdings, in 1996 with the aim of capturing a higher share in the primary securities market of Hong Kong- and

China-based securities issuers. It is hardly doubted that in spite of the loss of the former monopoly position in cross-border financing for China, the BOC is set to remain the leading Chinese bank in international markets. As a domestic player in China, the bank remains considerably smaller than behemoths such as the ICBC, which boasts more than twice the local staff of the BOC. The Bank of China rating from Moody's is Baa1, while Standard & Poor's assigns a BBB rating to the bank. Something of a stir was created in 1995, when Moody's downgrade of the BOC rating from A3 to Baa1, triggered by the bank "commercialisation" process in China, resulted in the cancellation of a HK$5bn floating rate certificate of deposit issue of the BOC because of pricing problems.

INDUSTRIAL AND COMMERCIAL BANK OF CHINA

The Industrial and Commercial Bank of China is most clearly the relic of the former PBOC commercial banking operations. It is today China's main savings haven, and its principal small- and medium-sized business lender. The development of the ICBC is a reflection of China's banking reform itself. Until 1995, its president, Ms Zhang Xiao, used to stress the high political responsibilities of the bank when she lauded the "pleasant memories of reform and development" in China and emphasised that ICBC's loan portfolio, largely dictated by the central government, was "under control". Today, burdened with a massive stock of non-performing loans but free to expand into formerly untouched business areas, the ICBC is struggling to become a more profitable commercial retail bank. It is now encouraged by its shareholder, the Chinese state, to conduct foreign exchange operations on both sides of the balance sheet, to engage in personal mortgage financing and to promote the sophistication of the Chinese payment system through ATMs and credit card issuing. By the end of 1995, the ICBC operated some 3,500 ATMs throughout the country and had a full 170 branches conducting international business. It is increasingly involved in international trade finance, but it still faces an uphill task in adapting to international standards of conduct. The annual reports of the ICBC do not contain more than two pages of explanatory notes to the balance sheet and profit and loss statement, leaving outside observers incapable of assessing the bank's performance over time. In 1995, one of its branches refused to honour a letter of credit for no obvious reasons, reminding foreign bankers of the immense task which the management and transformation of a former central plan bank of the size of the ICBC must pose. ICBC's long-term rating from Moody's is Baa1, one notch below China's sovereign rating of A3, and the bank is rated BBB by Standard & Poor's.

STATE DEVELOPMENT BANK

After a little less than three years in the market, the State Development Bank, which took over the policy lending functions formerly executed by the ICBC and the CCB, accumulated some US$38bn in assets by the end of 1996. Although the SDB had only acquired a relatively small loan porfolio from state-owned commercial banks in 1994 and often had to act through the CCB as its agent, it was already financing some 400 large- and medium-sized projects in China by January 1997. By these measures, it has become the most important of the three policy banks for the execution of the Chinese government's investment programmes. This perception was underlined by Moody's, which rated the bank's long-term foreign currency debt A3, and Standard & Poor's, which lifted SDB's initial rating of BBB to BBB+ in step with an upgrading of China's sovereign rating to BBB+ in May 1997. These top ratings have made the SDB a perfect vehicle for the Chinese government to raise foreign currency funds for infrastructure development abroad. In 1995 alone, the SDB raised over US$2.4bn in syndicated loans abroad, more than any other Chinese borrower, including the BOC. According to Xinhua News Agency, the total of international loans borrowed by SDB reached US$3.4bn by the beginning of 1997, the proceeds of which were mainly used to fund the Three Gorges Dam and the Qinshan Nuclear Power Plant, besides some 16 smaller projects. The breakthrough in international recognition, however, occurred in January 1997 when the SDB issued a 10-year US$300mn Yankee bond, which yielded no more than 80 basis points over the 10-year US Treasury bond, to fund the controversial Three Gorges project. Despite the bank's obligation to fund

SOEs and projects with often uncertain or dismal profitability outlooks, its management can be expected to exhibit more ambitious expansion plans in terms of local and foreign currency operations in the medium term. The posting of a US$10mn profit for 1996 and the publication of the fact that SDB had successfully recalled 87%, or US$3.8bn, of its outstanding interest payments and principal repayments in that year underlines the importance that the bank is attaching to its image in the international financial markets.

BANK OF COMMUNICATIONS

BOCOM, which holds a slightly weaker rating of Baa2 by Moody's, is widely seen as a leading second-tier bank. It was established in 1908 with the original goal being to direct financial funds to projects related to transport and communications development. The bank split in two after 1949, with one part moving to Taiwan, where the bank is now known as Chiao Tung Bank, and the other part being absorbed by the PBOC monobank. Only in 1987 the Chinese BOCOM was re-opened as a state-owned bank with a new head office in Shanghai. Its mission was to develop into a leading sectoral player with a focus on the economic modernisation of the country. By the end of 1995, the bank ranked fifth in China behind the Big Four, with total assets of approximately US$43bn. Though ultimately controlled by the central government and answerable directly to the State Council, BOCOM is more independent than the other state-owned banks. Its regional operations are named as branches, but actually constitute subsidiaries in which regional governments hold certain equity participations. It is believed that the stake of the central government in BOCOM had fallen to around 20% by the middle of the 1990s. The two major strengths of the bank are its dominant position in the booming Shanghai area and its comparably smaller exposure to weak SOEs. In August 1995, BOCOM was the only one of five Chinese banks to receive a D+ Bank Financial Strength Rating by Moody's, while the stand-alone financial strength of the BOC was rated D and the three other specialised commercial banks, the ABC, ICBC and PBOC, only got away with an E+ rating.

BOCOM is currently venturing more aggressively into foreign markets and it may soon increase its modest branch network overseas.

HUA XIA BANK

Hua Xia Bank is an interesting example of a small and relatively young commercial bank with a dynamic history. The bank was founded in June 1992 by the giant Shougang Corporation (Capital Steel and Iron Corporation), then one of China's flagship SOEs, only months after Deng Xiaoping visited the company's steel mill and emphasised the importance of Shougang for the state economy. After being run for three years by the industrial parent enterprise, Hua Xia Bank suddenly announced a major restructuring in the second half of 1995 with the goal of converting itself into a joint-stock commercial bank. The bank's capital was raised from the equivalent of US$120mn to US$300mn, with Shougang's stake being diluted to about 20% and another 32 principally state-owned firms acquiring the balance of the bank's equity capital. While officially the restructuring occurred because Hua Xia Bank had accumulated significant inherent risks by being tied to one industrial shareholder, and because the new Commercial Bank Law encouraged non-state commercial banks to compete on a national basis with the four major specialised banks, it was more widely believed that the true reasons were political. The first word of the imminent shareholder shake-up came around five months after the resignation of Shougang's long-time chairman Zhou Guanwu, whose son Zhou Beifang, for his part chairman of Shougang's Hong Kong-listed Shougang Concord International and Shougang Concord Grand subsidiaries, was arrested one day before over mysterious allegations of commercial wrong-doings. At that time, the fall of Zhou Beifang and his father, a close ally of Deng Xiaoping, was highly publicised in the overseas media and interpreted as a sign of the waning influence of China's paramount leader. Unimpressed by the fundamental shake-up, Hua Xia Bank profited from the capital boost by aggressively expanding its loan portfolio from a level of US$672mn at end-1995 to US$1.2bn by the end of 1996. Headquartered in Beijing and operating with only two branches in Nanjing and Hangzhou until recently, it opened a Shanghai branch in late 1996 and now plans to add Jinan, Suzhou and Wenzhou to its network. Hua Xia Bank's transformation from a closely-held group subsidiary to a joint-stock commercial bank with national ambitions has so far been judged a success. The Everbright Bank followed suit in late 1996, when it reduced the former 100% control of the China Everbright Group to 51%, issued 3% of its total equity to the Asian Development Bank and allowed another 129 mainly state-owned Chinese firms to take a stake in its capital. China Investment Bank and CITIC Industrial Bank have let it be known in 1997 that they also envisage such a move towards a joint-stock commercial bank before long.

Appendix 4B: Foreign Banks in China

Table 4.2: The local presence of foreign banks in China

	Rep. offices	Branches	Subsidiaries	JVs[1]	Total
1978	0	5	0	0	5
1981	21	5	0	0	26
1985	148	22	0	0	170
1991	217	41	3	1	262
1992	192	70	3	7	272
1993	208	82	5	8	303
1994	294	99	9	6	408

[1] Only Sino-foreign joint ventures.

Sources: Reynolds (1982), Wilson (1986), Almanac of China's Finance and Banking (1992, 1993, 1994, 1995), PBOC (1995).

Appendix 4C: Funding for Chinese corporates

Methods by which funding was raised (figure 4.1), and the respective amounts (table 4.3).

4.1: Sources of outside funding for Chinese corporates in the mid-1990s

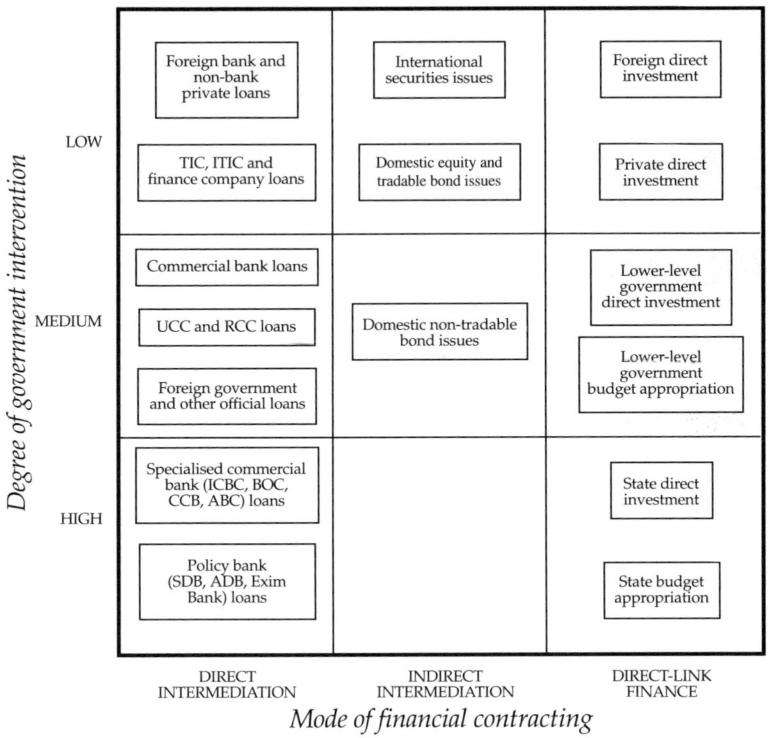

Table 4.3: Aggregated use of selected financing channels in China during 1990–95 (in US$bn)

Financial resources raised in domestic capital markets	bond issues	102.2
	equity issues	5.3
Financial resources raised abroad	bank loans	41.3
	non-bank private loans	5.4
	government and official loans	26.4
	bonds (including convertible)	9.8
	equity issues (B, H, N shares)	5.6
	direct investment	117.8

Sources: Calculations based on CSRC (1995), China Statistical Yearbook (1995), World Bank (1997), Kerry Securities Research Database, Euromoney Loanware & Noteware Database, Capital DATA Bondware Database, Shanghai Stock Exchange, Shenzhen Stock Exchange.

CHAPTER 5

CITIC Beijing

Simon Cartledge

The China International Trust and Investment Corp (CITIC) group is one of China's highest profile groups and remains a far more complex and mature group than other Chinese companies. We have conducted our study on two levels, the holding company and the listed company. This chapter looks at CITIC Beijing and some issues related to the Hong Kong listed company, CITIC Pacific. The following chapter focuses on CITIC Pacific from the point of view of its principal operations and investments.

The political divisions of the group, in general, fall along the lines of CITIC Beijing and the camp of Wang Jun, the group Chairman, and CITIC (HK) and CITIC Pacific, in the camp of Larry Yung, Chairman of CITIC Pacific. At least part of CITIC Beijing (the part associated with Wan Jun) is believed to be aligned with army interests, while CITIC (HK)'s interests generally fall more in line with a cadre of professional managers, both Chinese and non-Chinese. At the same time, CITIC Pacific's alignment with Larry Yung is evident from the destination of mainland investments, which are typically focused on the Shanghai area. Larry Yung is a native of Wuxi, Jiangsu province, an area just to the northwest of Shanghai.

China International Trust and Investment Corp is routinely defined as the reddest of China's red chips, one of China's few top companies, possibly even the best of all China's leading companies, a probable multinational. It undoubtedly has high name recognition. Hong Kong's *Far Eastern Economic Review* described the company in 1993 as "China's most spectacular economic success of the past decade", while Wardley James Capel (now HSBC James Capel) in its *Red Chips Directory (1993)* described the company's Hong Kong-listed arm, CITIC Pacific, as the "only true red chip" among the stocks making up the Hang Seng Index.

5.1: CITIC Group

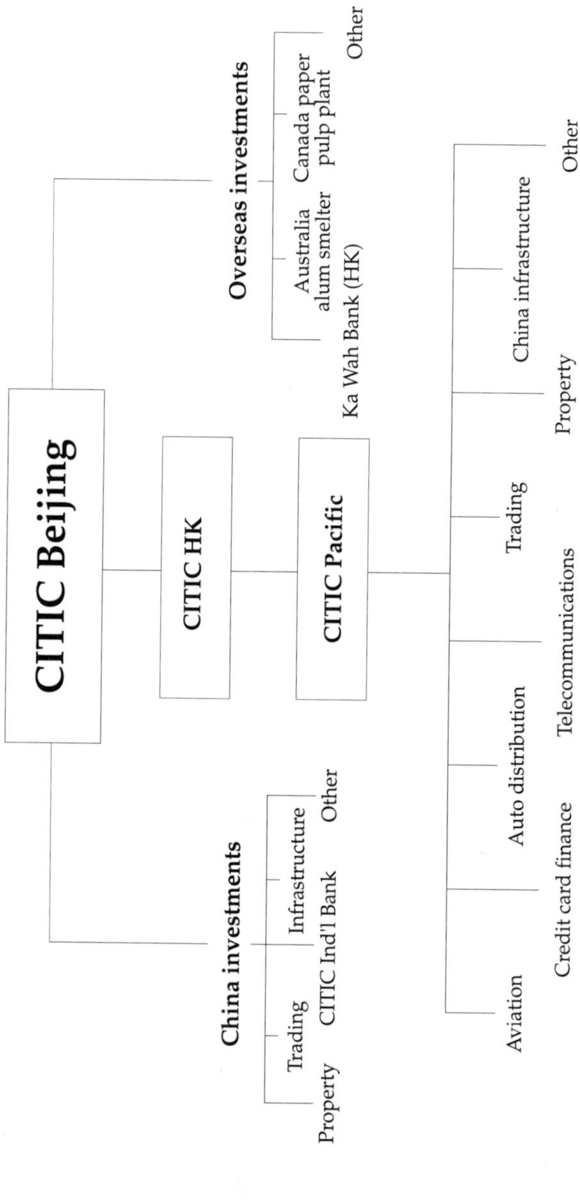

It also has some of the right qualifications. Take its assets, for example. As of October 1996, total assets stood at Rmb200bn (about US$24bn), according to Yao Jinrong, one of CITIC's executive directors (see table 5.1). Pretty good going for a company founded only 16 years earlier. Including overseas staff, it has 60,000 employees, working for a total of just under 40 subsidiaries and affiliated businesses. In China it is a partner in various Sino-foreign joint ventures. Abroad, it is China's largest overseas investor, accounting, according to the *Financial Times*, for about 20% of all the country's foreign investments (*Financial Times*, 16 March 1995).

Table 5.1
CITIC's year-end assets (Rmb bn)

1990	33.8
1991	45.3
1992	50.7
1993	82.9
1994	135.5
1995	166.7
1996	200.0 (October 1996)

Sources: CITIC, Moody's Investors Service

But the company has also tripped up several times. Its most embarrassing moment to date was the revelation in 1994 of losses of US$40mn on the London Metals Exchange, sustained through unauthorised futures trading by CITIC staff, and which at first the company was unwilling to pay for (see later in this chapter). At the same time its performance has also been less than startling. Its pre-tax profits have only really been worthy of note since 1993, when they hit Rmb3.4bn; before that they were a relatively insignificant few hundred million renminbi a year. The last two years (for which data were available at the time of writing) have seen reasonable performances, Rmb2bn (US$193) in 1994 and Rmb2.4bn (US$241mn) in 1995, neither as strong as 1993 (see table 5.2 below). Potentially more worrying is its debt to asset ratio, which in 1995 stood at 89.8%.

Table 5.2
CITIC's pre-tax profits, 1989–95 (Rmb bn)

1989	245
1990	259
1991	369
1992	380
1993	3,351
1994	2,012
1995	2,431

Source: Moody's Investors Service,
CITIC Annual Report 1995

Putting performance aside, two other factors look as if they might undermine the company's long-term prospects. First, the way CITIC's goals have been both vaguely defined and constantly changing, on occasion appearing to be driven by a mixture of whim and opportunism, has prevented it from developing a coherent strategy over any period beyond the short term. And second, the fading of Deng Xiaoping's influence in the mid-1990s left its much-vaunted connections looking decidedly disconnected, and possibly even detrimental to its financial health (as is argued in the case of Cathay Pacific below).

Both of these problems are surmountable. Indeed, the company seems be trying to overcome the first by turning itself primarily into a financial conglomerate, while the second can be overcome by virtue of being a "good" company, one that is well-managed, relying upon its own internal skills and talents rather than the connections of its top officials with China's political leaders. Here there is also cause for hope. CITIC has managed, so far at least, to avoid some of the worst problems that have befallen companies granted rights to go out and do business for China. Capital Iron & Steel Corporation (Shougang), a Beijing-based steel firm that has branched into everything from banking to Hong Kong investments, and China Everbright, a conglomerate originally similar in its aspirations to CITIC, are two examples that spring to mind.

Both companies, like CITIC, rose because their leaders had strong connections to Deng Xiaoping and so were granted the freedom to invest both inside and outside China with fairly few restraints. Both made poor business decisions. Shougang, for example, paid a way-over-the-top US$312mn for an iron mine in Peru and attempted to establish itself as a major conglomerate in Hong Kong. Running out of money fast, it twice called on the government for emergency loans, before finally coming unstuck in 1995 when Zhou Beifang, the son of its head, Zhou Guanwu, and the person in charge of the company's Hong Kong operations, was arrested for corruption. Little was heard of the affair until late 1996, though it retains its domestic importance as a steel maker. Everbright has fared worse because, with the exception of a bank, it has no true business to fall back on. After a glowing start when it was talked of in the same terms as CITIC, a series of poor business decisions left it in a complete mess by the end of the 1980s. Although it has restructured since then, it has yet to show signs of acting as a substantial corporate force.

Compared with both these firms, CITIC appears a paragon. But is it really? A lot depends on what is meant. Well-managed? Well-managed by international standards? Well-managed by the standards of state-owned enterprises in China? Other questions related to CITIC's quality turn around how well it succeeds in doing what it sets out to do, whether it has succeeded in developing expertise, or whether it is still too dependent on patronage. Finally, the most important question, will it continue to thrive? Or to put the same question another way, where will CITIC be at the end of the decade? What follows is a sketch of the main incidents of CITIC's brief history with the goal of drawing out key themes, the most significant being that CITIC, despite its elevated status among Chinese firms, remains essentially a state-owned Chinese firm, with the few advantages and many disadvantages this brings with it.

History

How did CITIC first rise to pre-eminence, and then slip back to its current status of important but not quite leading corporation? According to popular legend, the company was launched on the personal initiative of Deng Xiaoping, who asked a former Shanghai capitalist Rong Yiren to come up with ways of bringing technology and capital into China; Mr Rong returned a month later and suggested CITIC. As a result, CITIC was founded in October 1979 with just Rmb30mn of capital, 20 people working in three rented hotel suites and the vaguest of mandates — to import technology and management expertise, conduct economic and technological cooperation at home and abroad, and establish domestic and international financial and trading business. Its initial capital was from the Ministry of Finance, and the Rmb30mn expanded to Rmb600mn of seed capital.

Since then, its history can broadly be divided into four phases,

1. 1979 to mid-1980s: establishes itself in China.
2. 1987 to early 1990s: reorganised; establishes itself in Hong Kong and elsewhere overseas.
3. Early 1990s: moves heavily into finance and strategic investments; more management changes.
4. Mid-1990s: loses its way amidst a sea of investment possibilities.

Establishment: 1979 to early 1980s

CITIC's first few years were eventful, but on a relatively small scale. In 1982, for example, it had an income of just Rmb26.5mn, then about US$14mn. This had trebled by 1984, but still left it as a relatively small company. Size, however, should not be equated with significance. In 1982, it became the first Chinese borrower since 1949 to issue international debt, with a yen-denominated straight bond. Even more significant were the institutional ties it was laying down. In 1984 it was granted the status of being a "ministry-level company under the central government", meaning that it reported directly to the State Council, China's cabinet, as ministries do. Among the other organisations with this status are the People's Bank of China. Only a handful of other Chinese companies have this status. Furthermore, being a state-owned firm, it cannot be declared bankrupt.

Reorganisation: CITIC establishes itself overseas

By the middle of the 1980s CITIC had established a reasonable footing, but a relatively small-scale portfolio. The big change in the company's development came with a couple of reorganisations, first in 1986, followed by another in 1987, since which it has conducted all its business activities through subsidiaries. These changes allowed the company to start making a name for itself above all by investing overseas, especially in Hong Kong, and by becoming heavily financially focused. In 1986 CITIC took over Hong Kong's Ka Wah Bank after the bank ran into trouble over its loan portfolio. The following year saw its business further expand with the establishment of CITIC Industrial Bank.

Ka Wah Bank has remained directly in the hands of CITIC in Beijing. Of far more importance was the founding in early 1987 of CITIC Hong Kong as its wholly-owned subsidiary, and under which all its Hong Kong activities were consolidated. (It had previously been represented in the territory by an office established in 1980.)

The events of June 1989 in Beijing, when the Chinese government sent the army into the city to crush the pro-democracy movement, caused problems for CITIC. In the immediate aftermath of the protests, an official investigation of CITIC's activities uncovered unauthorised foreign currency transactions, tax evasion and profiteering. The company was fined Rmb19mn (then about US$5mn), and several senior government figures were forced to give up honorary directorships, among them the current vice-premier Zhu Rongji and the children of high party officials, including Deng Zhifang, one of Deng Xiaoping's sons.

The fine was really nothing more than a slap on the wrist. Clearly the company felt no need to restrain its activities, especially in Hong Kong, where CITIC Hong Kong went on a spending spree, buying up stakes in several leading companies (notably 20% of Hongkong Telecom) perceived to be underpriced because of the reaction to the riots and their aftermath in Beijing. Within one four-month period the company increased its assets by 400% to well over HK$10bn (about US$1.28bn).

CITIC's growth, however, was not leading to huge profitability. Turnover in 1989 was Rmb2.2bn. Profits that year were just Rmb245mn (then about US$65mn), only growing 5% in 1990 to Rmb258mn, though picking up quite a bit in 1991 to Rmb368mn. What the company was doing, however, was laying the foundation in Hong Kong for the establishment of a business empire that, in size at least, would start to rival that of the colony's large conglomerates or *hongs*. The next step down this route was the founding in 1990 of CITIC's publicly listed arm, CITIC Pacific, after CITIC Hong Kong acquired a controlling stock in the already-listed Tyfull Co Ltd and renamed it.

CITIC Pacific, which is currently owned about 45% by CITIC Hong Kong, now holds stakes in a number of key businesses in Hong Kong, notably:

- Cathay Pacific, which CITIC owned 25% of in late 1996
- Dragonair
- Hongkong Telecom
- Macau Telecom
- Dah Chong Hong
- Cross Harbour Tunnel
- Property, notably a 50% stake in Hong Kong Resort Co Ltd, the developers of the Discovery Bay residential housing complex on Lantau Island.

After all the excitement in Hong Kong in the early 1990s, CITIC turned its gaze back on China in the second half of 1992, possibly spurred on by the decision in August to grant it powers to make investments worth up to Rmb200mn (then US$37mn) in China and US$30mn overseas without having to seek government permission. The outburst of activity was not surprising, coming as it did in the wake of Deng Xiaoping's now all but mythic "southern tour" of February and March 1992 when he launched China onto a spectacular boom through the following couple of years.

In November 1992 CITIC signed letters of intent for the development of Daxie Island, a previously fairly insignificant island just off the coast of Ningbo in Zhejiang province, with the Zhejiang provincial government and Ningbo city government. The same month, CITIC Hong Kong signed deals in Shanghai for a 4x300 MW power station in Pudong, a road tunnel under the Huangpu River, industrial redevelopment in Pudong and Shanghai city centre, and a container terminal. This burst of domestic-focused activity called for more finance. So in January 1993, CITIC Hong Kong sold its 12% stake in Hongkong Telecom to CITIC Pacific for HK$10.4bn, making a HK$4bn profit in the process. Not that CITIC Pacific was worried: it picked the shares up at a 20% discount to the market, and paid for them, plus power plants in Jiangsu and Henan provinces, with a HK$7.1bn share issue.

In retrospect, this can be seen as the heyday of CITIC's financial and business juggling. The same year, Rong Yiren stepped down as chairman to become China's vice president. His replacement, Wei Mingyi, had first joined CITIC as a vice president in 1985. Mr Wei had secured a masters' degree from Brown University in the USA in 1949, and subsequently risen through China's bureaucracy at the Ministry of Electronics Industry, where as vice-minister he worked closely with China's current president Jiang Zemin. He was regarded as a surprise choice when he took over from Rong Yiren — even then Wang Jun, Mr Wei's eventual successor, was seen as a more likely candidate — and it was suggested he would lack both the clout and connections of his predecessor. Then again, who could have had the same?

Focus on finance and more changes

Mr Wei started with a bang, announcing a month after taking up his new post his plans for the Daxie Island project. Despite this talk of a domestic project, however, during his chairmanship the one thing that soared above all was CITIC's foreign assets. Indeed, even Mr Wei himself does not seem to have appreciated how fast these had the potential to increase: in October 1994, a little over a year into his reign, the *China Daily* cited Wei Mingyi as saying CITIC's asset value would grow to Rmb120bn (US$14bn) by 2000, up from the Rmb83bn (US$9.6bn) of the end of 1993 (itself a huge hike from the Rmb50.7bn of the end of 1992). In fact, CITIC had way surpassed this figure as early as the end of 1994, only three months after Mr Wei had announced the target, suggesting, if nothing else, that CITIC may have dubious internal account keeping methods.

Such growth, however, would not be enough to keep Mr Wei in his job. Within a few months of taking over his post, his position was seriously undermined by the announcement in early 1994 that CITIC's Shanghai subsidiary had run up losses of US$40mn in the unauthorised futures trading of metals, principally copper, on the London Metals Exchange. The losses arose because traders took advantage of special credit lines offered by LME brokers to the traders to cover discrepancies in timing between hedged positions in the futures market and the actual time when shipments were physically made (Reuters, 3 May 1995).

CITIC was at first distinctly ambivalent on whether it would repay the losses: as CITIC Shanghai is a subsidiary, it was under no legal obligation to do so. But four people, including the president of CITIC Shanghai, were reportedly detained by the police, and by March 1995 CITIC announced it had reached an agreement with LME brokers over outstanding debts. The same month, and shortly after another the Shougang purge, Mr Wei tendered his resignation to the State Council and CITIC's board of directors.

Two months later, in May, Wang Jun (then 54) was finally appointed chairman. Mr Wang's former post, of president, was handed to Qin Xiao (then 49). Mr Wang, the son of former Long Marcher and Deng Xiaoping ally Wang Zhen, who had died in 1993, was originally an engineering graduate form Harbin Military Engineering College. He worked in shipyards in Wuhan and Shanghai, and served in the navy before beginning his career at CITIC 16 years earlier in 1979 at its founding. Before taking up the chairmanship he had served as both vice-president, starting in 1986, board member from 1990, and president, and was the head of Continental Mariner, a Hong Kong-based shipowning and investment company owned by another Chinese firm, Poly Group Corp.

His immediate goal after taking over the helm was to take CITIC into insurance and financial services because of problems the company had making money from the (largely state-run) industrial sector. To this end CITIC set up a securities business in June 1995 which brought together about 20 securities firms already owned by CITIC with the announced goal of creating an investment bank (and to try and run its subsidiaries better in the wake of the LME fiasco), and talked about beefing up CITIC Industrial Bank, which, although accounting for around half of CITIC's assets, only had eight branches (Beijing, Dalian, Qingdao, Jinan, Hangzhou, Nanjing, Shenzhen and Shanghai) in early 1995.

These plans were not exactly new. The *China Daily* in October 1994 cited Wei Mingyi as saying the company was awaiting approval from the People's Bank of China to set up a life insurance company and was preparing to merge its 18 securities business departments into a new securities company which would act solely as a broker and an underwriter, and would not trade shares for itself. But they were quickly turned on their head when CITIC in the second half of 1995 and early 1996 began setting itself up, most visibly through CITIC Pacific, as a China infrastructure play. CITIC Pacific did this by selling down its stakes in Hongkong Telecom and Cathay Pacific

Confusion over investment strategy

Although this was not the first time CITIC had made an about-face on its long-term investment strategy, CITIC Pacific managing director Henry Fan Hung-ling announced in August 1993 that CITIC Hong Kong would be taking part in a US$1bn toll tunnel in Shanghai, acquisition of 10mn square feet of property in Shanghai and a huge oil exploration venture as part of moves to make CITIC Pacific far more of an infrastructure stock. It did seem to mark a change of direction as well as a calling home of the prodigal son. Indeed, it was perhaps a touch ironic, as over the years CITIC has been criticised for preferring to seek greater returns overseas rather than using the money it made there to investing in its home, and so meet the goals it had originally been set up for. Of course, the money abroad, or at least in Hong Kong has always tended to do far better, certainly in the shorter term, not least because of the lack of constraints on what are the "correct" businesses for CITIC to invest in.

For example, contrast its relative success in Hong Kong with its China business. This is very much a mixed kettle of fish. Its highest profile project, among 300 or so ventures, is the development of Zhejiang province's Daxie Island in partnership with American engineering and construction firm Bechtel. Despite much fanfare, however, this project is questionable on various basic grounds. Not the least is why do it in Ningbo at all? True, the city has a few advantages such as a deepwater port, and it loosely falls in the orbit of Shanghai-region network cities, but investing so heavily in it at such an undeveloped stage is a statement of hope even more than of intent.

Table 5.3
CITIC'S assets as percent of total assets

Finance (inc. CITIC Industrial Bank)	73%
Industrial	10%
Property	6%
Telecommunications	4%
Commerce, trade and services	4%
Transportation, roads and bridges	3%

Source: CITIC Annual Report 1995

Table 5.4
Breakdown of CITIC's industrial assets

Raw materials	64%
Energy	17%
Automotive and machinery	12%
Others	7%

Source: CITIC Annual Report 1995

CITIC's other major domestic investments fall into similar categories. It has various automotive and machinery projects. The most recent of these to be unveiled was Zhengzhou Nissan Corp, a Rmb620mn (US$74mn) car plant at Zhengzhou in Henan province in partnership with Nissan, which in May 1996 began production of vans. CITIC has said it will invest Rmb3bn (US$360mn) in the plant over the next five years, by which time vehicle output will have risen from its current capacity of 60,000 to 180,000 annually, with some 100,000 engines also being manufactured there. This project, of course, is unproven, and may eventually turn out to be very successful. But another CITIC car venture, however, has proved less successful. It has a stake in the Guangzhou Peugeot joint venture, largely controlled by the Guangzhou municipal government and which has proved a total fiasco.

Other schemes have even more dubious pasts. The most notorious of the these is the No 541 Machinery Plant in the northwestern province of Shanxi. This was a large tank-manufacturing plant that CITIC took over, or perhaps more accurately had foisted upon it, in 1988 with the goal of converting it to civilian production. CITIC, however, was not allowed to dismiss any of the plant's 20,000 work force and officials blocked investment in new machinery. In an interview with Hong Kong's *South China Morning Post* newspaper in August 1993 Wei Mingyi said after five years of loss-making under CITIC the plant was still not breaking even, though he hoped it would in 1994. It is not known whether 541 has turned the corner yet.

Power is another area where the track record is mixed. Through Sunburst Energy Development Corp, in which CITIC has a controlling interest, it has arranged financing and construction of Jiangsu province's Ligang Power Plant, Inner Mongolia's No 1 Baotou Power Plant and Henan province's Zhengzhou Power Plant. It is now developing second phases at Zhengzhou and Ligang, and a plant at Jiaxing power station (150 kilometres from Daxie Island). Then there are its chemical interests, which include the Yizheng Chemical Fibre Plant in Jiangsu province, in which CITIC had a 30% stake until its holding was diluted when Yizheng was floated on the Hong Kong Stock Exchange in 1994. We also have its telecoms business, with firms making cellular telephones, paging systems and switches, plus, since the establishment of China's second network carrier, China United Communications (Unicom, also known as Liantong), stakes in mobile phone networks across the country. On top of this are satellites via an effective 24% holding in the Hong Kong-based Asia Satellite Communications Co, founded in 1988. ASIASAT currently owns two satellites, which were launched in 1990 and 1995.

If this array of businesses was not confusing enough, one has to turn next to CITIC's overseas holdings. As mentioned above (and according to the *South China Morning Post*, 14 March 1995), CITIC is China's largest overseas investor, with about 18–20% of all China's overseas investments. These investments are, like most of CITIC's businesses interests, diverse. They range from CITIC Australia, whose own diversification (meat to aluminium, plus being the vehicle to buy a 10% stake in Hong Kong-based retailer Yaohan) has made it one of Australia's 300 biggest firms, to CITIC Canada, whose main investment is a pulp mill, through the intermediary of a steel mill and logging mill at opposite ends of the United States, CITIC Europa (which has a joint venture with an

Italian clothing firm making cashmere garments in Inner Mongolia) and manufacturing operations in Thailand.

It looks like the question is what sectors has CITIC not said at one time or another it would be becoming involved in. For example, in April 1993, the same month he took over the chairmanship from Rong Yiren, Wei Mingyi announced his plans for the company. As well as its involvement in Daxie Island, he also listed securities, insurance, futures, petroleum, telecommunications and aviation. Not a bad list, especially when considering that it ignores most of the biggest sectors and industries that the company was already in.

The trouble with investing domestically, and in non-financial sectors, however, is that it is not where CITIC has made money. Speaking in an interview with a Chinese news agency, company chairman Wang Jun said that 80% of CITIC's profits in 1995 were generated by its overseas investment. He added that despite only generating 20% of the firm's profits, its domestic investments accounted for 50% of all its investments. And it was still moving further down this finance-related road: building up its securities business into an investment bank, expanding CITIC Industrial Bank, whose assets reached Rmb86bn (US$10.4bn) and branch network grew to 17 in 1995, and entering the insurance and fund management sectors.

Discussion and conclusion

The way in which CITIC is treated as the blue chip of red chips is misleading. Its history has been far from trouble free, ranging from being found guilty of various crimes in the wake of June 1989 to the US$40mn it lost on the London Metals Exchange. It may not be treated as an economic dumping ground any more, as it was when it was saddled with No 541 Machinery Plant, but it is treated as subservient to greater needs. Furthermore its strategy remains as blurred as ever. Certainly it has a mission to "help China" in various ways, but its view of what this means has rarely extended beyond the current deal. Finally, its much-vaunted connections are as double-edged as ever. The very closeness of some of the ties, such as CITIC Pacific's chairman, Larry Yung, the son of Rong Yiren, or the current chairman, Wang Jun, the son of Deng

Xiaoping's close associate Wang Zhen (died in 1993), means that with Mr Deng's physical decline and, finally, death in February 1997, the company is left looking naked.

Nonetheless, this does not mean CITIC should be written off. Rather the question is to what degree it will continue to be successful in the future. Interesting points are the many things it has started but never taken to their conclusion. Take, for example, CITIC Industrial Bank. When CITIC took over Ka Wah Bank in Hong Kong, which had some US branches, it was suggested that CITIC might be able to build on this foundation. However, nothing much has happened since then. CITIC Industrial Bank's total assets in 1989 were Rmb15.8bn (then US$4.2bn), Ka Wah Bank's assets were HK$11bn (US$1.4bn). As mentioned above, at the end of 1995, CITIC Industrial Bank's total assets had grown to Rmb86bn, while Ka Wah Bank's reserves stood at HK$154mn (US$20mn) and its post-tax profits for the year at HK$319mn (US$41mn), both still petty on an international scale.

On the positive side is CITIC's role as a pioneer on the world's financial markets, ranging from its issuance of a yen-denominated straight bond in 1982, making it the first Chinese borrower since 1949 to issue international debt anywhere in the world, to July 1993 when it launched the first Yankee bond by a Chinese borrower in the American public debt market since 1949. Unfortunately, more recently things have proved trickier. The most notable incident on its financial side was the autumn 1995 downgrading of the company by American investment rating firm Moody's. This put CITIC on a par with China's state-owned banks, which were downgraded in April of the same year. Since then, CITIC's ratings have remained at Baa1 for long-term debt and Prime-3 for short-term debt. Paradoxically, it is unlikely to improve on these while China continues moving towards a more market-driven economy. The reason CITIC and the state-owned banks had their previous higher ratings was because their borrowings were perceived as sovereign debt; the more the government distances itself from state-owned entities in an attempt to make them more commercial, the more vulnerable they look. Only by improving the nature of their business, and becoming transparent enough for investors to see this improvement, will CITIC and other Chinese financial institutions be able to push up their ratings once again.

Another big question mark hangs over the ability of Wang Jun, presuming he remains at the head of CITIC. At the time of writing rumours had been circulating in Beijing that he was unlikely to stay at the head of CITIC or, if he did, to become no more than a figurehead. Certainly Mr Wang cut a rather poor figure in his first year at the helm, especially when compared with CITIC's founder, Rong Yiren, the man "widely credited with turning CITIC into the sprawling multibillion-dollar business empire that it is today", according to the *Far Eastern Economic Review.*

But then what exactly did Mr Rong bring to the party? His most outstanding achievement was his getting CITIC the freedom to make its own decisions without having to refer them back to government officials, in particular the right in 1992 to sign investments worth up to Rmb200mn (then US$37mn) in China and US$30mn overseas. CITIC still has this freedom, but its very success has left it more beholden to the powers above it. There is no better example of this than the hoops CITIC was forced to jump through over its stake in the Hong Kong-based airline Cathay Pacific in early 1996. The year before, CITIC had reduced its stake in the airline, which was then majority owned by British trading conglomerate Swire, from 12% to 10%. This was followed in early 1996 by the resignations of Larry Yung and Henry Fan from Cathay's board, apparently to let CITIC distance itself from the British-owned airline which was vociferously opposing a bid by China National Aviation Corp (both China's aviation regulator and the owner of China's national airline, Air China) to set up its own airline in Hong Kong as a rival to Cathay. In April, however, it raised its stake to 25% when the ownership of Cathay and Hong Kong's other airline, Dragonair, was reshuffled to give CNAC a major stake in Dragonair. The manner in which the deal was carried out suggested that CITIC had nothing like the independence it had had a few years earlier to make decisions principally on commercial grounds.

CITIC falls directly under the State Council and in its heyday it behaved like a wayward province, determined to set its own course and establish the maximum amount of economic freedom possible. And much as the central government has striven to rein in regions such as Guangdong that have gone too far off on their own, so the current conservative leadership has wanted to do the same to CITIC. Larry Yung's public declaration in December 1995 that Chinese interference after 1997 could "kill Hong Kong" cannot have been popular with the central government. Not surprisingly, given the conservative nature of most of China's current top leadership, the favoured enterprises are, arguably, the big state-owned conglomerates, the automotive, steel and petrochemical giants such as China National Chemicals Import-Export Corp (Sinochem) and China National Aviation Corp. These companies also have their eyes set on international expansion. They also have an added advantage: CITIC has grown as an investment holding without the type of influence that a company such as Shougang exercises over its industry, steel, and CITIC does not have the bloated bureaucracy most of these firms have built up over their decades of existence. But then it also does not appear to have developed the kinds of controls or discipline needed to establish Western-type business practices. Is it fair to ask which Chinese companies have? After all CITIC has no more access to the pool of trained Chinese managers than do foreign joint ventures. Their biggest problem is human resources, and CITIC's best people are quite likely to be targets for foreign-invested businesses. Though its internal management structure might be changing in the wake of the CITIC Shanghai/London Metals Exchange scandal, it is unlikely this will lead to the establishment of adequate controls over all its business. Indeed, a much more likely scenario is simply that the company as a whole will be subjected to greater overall political control.

Such a move would only perpetuate the continual problem CITIC faces in establishing a guiding strategy. Even CITIC Hong Kong, despite the acquisition of high-profile and promising investments, has long been considered nothing more than a holding vehicle for a collection of minority stakes in companies, that for the most part can be invested in directly on the open market. Admittedly many of these companies are in the Hong Kong blue-chip league, but if anything this makes it even more vulnerable to the accusation that CITIC does not add value, its name adds value.

If its name, or connections, are called into question, then it has little to fall back on.

As well as the lack of truly high-quality staff at CITIC's Headquarters in Beijing, it also has to be asked just how high the quality of its numerous business are. As remarked at the beginning, its debt-asset ratio in 1995 of 89.8% is high, and indeed it could well be worse than it sounds: given that half of CITIC's assets are in China, where assets are usually valued in a more arbitrary manner. For instance, if assets were to be valued too dearly, the ratio would almost certainly be over 100% if/when the scrutiny of Western accounting measures were to be applied.

CITIC is too important to disappear, barring some unforeseen event, but it is probably past its peak in the patronage-driven world of China business. It no longer looks like a dead certainty to be one of China's top ten firms, which it did in the early 1990s. It is worth asking whether it could move beyond being a "Dengist" creation and become a freestanding entity, but the answer is probably no, at least over the next five to ten years. As well as its declining support at the centre, it has no one breathing down its neck demanding a better performance. No one, that is, like shareholders, analysts, or the press. Rather than giving the company freedom this actually acts as a drag: it simply has no incentive to try to squeeze better performance out of its many different parts. Thus CITIC will almost certainly become a business whose parts will amount to much more than its whole: the obvious thing to do with such a business in the West, is split it up and sell off its divisions. At some point, if the Chinese government ever gets serious about privatisation, it will have few better places to start with than CITIC. In other words, the current forecast is for the company to keep growing, but perform anaemically, until some external force is allowed to redirect its growth.

CHAPTER 6

CITIC Pacific

Anil Daswani

The Beijing-backed CITIC group made its appearance in Hong Kong in January 1985 through the incorporation of Tylfull Company Limited. Tylfull was engaged in small-scale property investment and development projects in the (then) colony. A major restructuring exercise transformed the group in 1990, when Tylfull acquired from CITIC (Hong Kong) a 38% interest in Hong Kong Dragon Airlines and two industrial buildings. Concurrently, CITIC (Hong Kong) acquired a 51% controlling interest in the group. During 1991 the group acquired a 12.5% stake in Cathay Pacific Airways for HK$2.9bn, a 20% interest in Macao Telecom for HK$250mn and changed its name to CITIC Pacific in August.

In 1992 CITIC Pacific increased its stake in Hong Kong Dragon Airways to 46% and acquired Hang Cheong, the holding company of its motor vehicle and food trading subsidiary, Dah Chong Hong. The group's largest investment was made during 1993 when CITIC Pacific acquired a 12% stake in Hong Kong Telecom from CITIC (Hong Kong). In the same year the group also took interests in two power station projects, a waste treatment plant, 10% of the Western Harbour Tunnel Company, 10% of Hong Kong Air Cargo Terminals Limited and a 55% stake in each of four manufacturing operations in the PRC. Acquisitions in 1994 included a 20% stake in Manhattan Card, a 50% interest in Hong Kong Resort Company, another 25% interest in Western Harbour Tunnel, 28.5% of the Eastern Harbour Tunnel Company and four bridges/tunnels in Shanghai. At the end of 1995 the group acquired additional interests in Shanghai infrastructure.

During 1995 and the early part of 1996, it appeared that CITIC had bowed to political pressure from Beijing. In a bid to distance itself from the British-controlled affiliates, Cathay Pacific and Hong Kong Telecom, CITIC sold stock in both counters. The group cut its stake in Hong Kong Telecom to 8% to raise funds for the investment in PRC infrastructure. Pressure from mainland-backed China National Aviation Corp (CNAC) to establish an airline in Hong Kong led to the group publicly stating that competition in the territory was inevitable. To add insult to injury, the group cut its stake in Cathay to 10% and removed senior staff from Cathay's board. At this stage the group was committed to develop Dragonair as its key aviation affiliate.

However, a surprise announcement in April 1996 led to the group back-pedalling on its previous views on Cathay. Swire Pacific, CITIC Pacific, Cathay Pacific and CNAC jointly issued a press release that completely changed the face of Hong Kong aviation. The crux of the deal allowed CNAC, China's aviation regulator, to acquire a 35.86% stake in Dragonair — 17.66% each from CITIC and Swire/Cathay and 0.55% from the Chao family. CNAC thus became the majority shareholder in Dragonair, with the stakes of CITIC, Swire and Cathay being reduced to 28.5%, 17.8% and 7.7% respectively.

CNAC appointed representatives to the board and executive committee of Dragonair in proportion to its shareholding. Cathay will continue to provide Dragonair with infrastructure and support for its operations.

Concurrent with the Dragonair deal, CITIC acquired an additional 15% stake in Cathay Pacific. The stake was acquired at a discount of almost 15% to the market, ensuring political harmony for the Swire empire.

CITIC Pacific is now regarded as China's flagship corporation in Hong Kong, and as the favoured and most liquid Chinese investment vehicle, employing over 10,000 staff of which 5,700 are in China.

Aviation interests

Cathay Pacific Airways, 25% stake (1996)
The Swire group, one of the leading conglomerates in Hong Kong, has played the political game for Hong Kong's skies skilfully, and has shown an uncanny ability to work with China and companies with ties to China. Besides selling its stake in Dragonair at a price advantageous to the Chinese parties, it placed 572.9mn new shares

of Cathay Pacific at HK$11.00 per share to CITIC Pacific. As Swire issued new shares for the placement, its stake in an enlarged Cathay fell to 43.9% from 52.6%, while CITIC's stake rose to 25% from 10%. CNAC, CITIC and China Travel all confirmed their support for the existing Cathay management, but they will appoint four members to the airline's board and two members to its executive committee. More importantly, all of the parties' major shareholders agreed to maintain their investment in Cathay for the long term. With CNAC focusing on Dragonair, and CITIC holding a more substantial stake in Cathay, there is no longer any political uncertainty surrounding Cathay. The airline has been trading at a huge discount in recent years as a result of concerns that Cathay would not maintain its near-monopoly over the Hong Kong skies after 1997.

The main factor that will continue to boost earnings is the growing demand in the region, which will outstrip the current capacity surge from both new airports and new start-up carriers. Over the past four years investors have hammered airline stocks because of a recession that has eroded the bottom line of all but the leanest of the carriers. In this regard, Asia is home to some of the world's most profitable carriers, namely Singapore Airlines and Cathay Pacific Airways.

The Asian airlines that have managed to stave off the red ink are those that have been successful in cutting costs, slowing capacity growth and capitalising on their lucrative routes. Cathay Pacific has been successful on all fronts having nearly completed its home-basing scheme and by introducing new pay scales for pilots. In addition, by increasing the average number of flying hours for a Cathay pilot from 550 to 700 per year, cost efficiencies improved dramatically. The airline is no longer recruiting any first officers and will allow the existing pilots to gradually increase the number of hours they fly in line with the growth from the new fleet. The upcoming new capacity is based on existing orders arriving over the next two years, and the airline has developed into the Asian hub for flights into both Japan and Taiwan. Although business from Cathay Pacific's lucrative destinations will continue to provide an excellent base for recurrent earnings, rising load factors and rising yields from Cathay's other destinations will also add significantly.

In 1995, Asian international traffic represented 22.2% of total world RPMs (Revenue Passenger Miles), and although it is only expected to rise to 28.1% of total RPMs by the end of 2005, RPMs will actually rise by nearly 88%. Cathay does not participate in the PRC domestic market and currently only participates in 20.1% of world RPMs. During 1990–95 Cathay has maintained a market share of between 6.69–6.99% of the Asian market and the addition of the US routes in 1996 will allow the airline to increase its market share to about 7.2% by the end of 1999. Our estimates of revenue are based on Cathay steadily increasing its position in the market.

The new Hong Kong airport at Chek Lap KoK with only one runway does not free up any prime slots, however, as it will operate 24 hours per day it will allow flexibility in deferring cargo flights, freeing up morning and evening slots. The new airport's first runway will have a capacity of 38 movements per hour, only a 22.6% improvement on the 31 hourly aircraft movements at the old airport, Kai Tak. The second runway's completion is expected in October 1998, five months after the opening of the airport. The capacity of Chek Lap Kok will then reach 60 aircraft movements per hour.

The current fears over new competition and deregulation have been dramatically over-played. With the existing forecasts for Asian growth the market can easily bear the arrival of new players. The current regulatory environment will survive for at least another 5–10 years. During this period, there is plenty of room for all of the Asian airlines to aggressively expand their fleets to capture the growth. However, it is only airlines that have planned in the early 1990s, that will be able to step up to the plate.

Hong Kong Dragon Airlines Limited, 25% stake (1997)

After the recent restructuring and an IPO expected in 1998, CITIC's stake in Dragonair will fall to 25% from 46% whilst Cathay's stake will fall from 30% to 14%. The airline operates scheduled and charter services to the PRC and Japan, however, the lack of new mainland slots has resulted in Dragonair flying to other smaller Southeast Asian airports. Before the restructuring was announced, the PRC did not award Dragonair any new slots as the airline has developed into the airline of choice in the PRC. Dragonair boasts load factors in the 90s whilst the local carriers such as China Eastern runs at loads in the 70s. Dragonair's routes allow the airline to boast some of the highest yields in the industry which has allowed high double-digit growth for the last four years.

The airline's fleet structure of seven A320s and three A330s is only suitable for short-haul regional routes. The fleet is currently the youngest in the world with an average age of only 1.5 years. Dragonair is set to benefit from both its current and new partners (particularly CNAC) by developing one of the most extensive networks between China and the region. This business would be significantly more profitable than the international routes currently served by Cathay Pacific. It is clear Cathay will retain its status as an international carrier, while Dragonair will focus on developing mainland business and smaller regional destinations. Upon listing, Dragonair is likely to be viewed as a leading red chip, but the counter will in effect be more on par with CITIC in that it is likely to be viewed as a blue chip. Dragonair reported net profit of HK$720mn in 1995, up almost 22% on 1994.

Hong Kong Air Cargo Terminal Limited (HACTL), 10% stake

At the end of 1993 CITIC acquired a 33.33% interest in Swire Aviation, whose sole asset is a 30% interest in HACTL, for a consideration of HK$120mn. Recently HACTL won the franchise to provide air cargo services at the new airport when it opens in 1998, however, the company will lose its monopoly status as a new competitor, Asia Airfreight Terminal Company, also received a franchise.

Telecommunications

Hong Kong Telecom, 8% stake (1996)

In a mid-1996 placement CITIC raised slightly over HK$3bn by disposing a 2% stake in Hong Kong Telecom (HKT) reducing their effective holding to 8%. Despite the cut, HKT still represented the largest portion, more than 20% of group's net asset value.

The telecom industry in Hong Kong is under severe pressure from competition from the new fixed line operators in the territory. In addition, HKT's lucrative international licence is due to expire in 2006. Speculation is mounting that HKT will relinquish its licence at an earlier date for a one-off payment from the government.

HKT's cellular dominance is also under threat as six new PCS licences were awarded at the end of September 1996. The winning bidders were Hutchison Telephone, Pacific Link, New World PCS, People's Telephone (backed by China Resources), Mandarin Communications (Lai Sun and USI Holdings) and P-Plus Link (Taiwan's Pacific Electric Wire & Cable). Hong Kong Telecom did not make the shortlist and many rumours of conspiracy against the British emerged. However, Telecom's bid was significantly higher than its competitors, as its pricing was similar to the group's existing GSM network.

The Office of the Telcommunications Authority has been keen to provide lower prices and improved services to the territory. It is believed that the winning tenders per-minute rates were between HK$0.70 and HK$1.00, significantly below the current HK$2.00 charged by Hong Kong Telecom. With Hong Kong cellular penetration currently at 16%, significantly higher than when the tenders were made, the new operators will have to play a new game and target the mass market. With a start-up expense of almost HK$1bn per PCS licence (each operator will need at least 200 base stations to operate a viable network), the new operators are expected to be aggressive on pricing to attract as much market share as possible.

With pressure on all of HKT's businesses, its FY95 results were disappointing. Although net profit rose 15.1%, operating profit only grew 13.4%. The growth in net profit came from an exceptional 82% rise in interest and other income. Growth in China traffic fell to 18% in FY95, from 30% over the past three years, due to the austerity programme, network congestion and an average 50% rise in service fees. No signs of improvement were on the horizon as of fall 1996.

Macau Telecom, 20% stake
Companhia de Telecomunicacoes de Macau SARL (CTM) is the sole provider of telecommunications in the Portuguese enclave. CTM's existing franchise expires on 31 December 2001. However, negotiations for an extension are already underway. CITIC's shareholding in CTM was acquired from CITIC (Hong Kong) in 1991 for HK$250mn and the investment has paid substantial dividends estimated at HK$72.5mn and HK$83.4mn in 1993 and 1994 respectively.

Trading & distribution

Dah Chong Hong
Dah Chong Hong (DCH) is a major Hong Kong–based trading company with substantial operations in the territory, the PRC, Japan, Canada and Singapore. Company operations are split between two key businesses: motor vehicles and trading. Most of the property assets of DCH have been transferred into CITIC's investment property portfolio enabling management to concentrate on its core trading and distribution activities.

Motor Vehicles — Hong Kong
DCH's motor business includes the distribution of motor vehicles, the provision of after-sale services and the sale of accessories and parts. The company represents Honda, Acura, Isuzu, Nissan, Nissan Diesel, Audi, Maserati, and Volkswagen in Hong Kong. In addition, the company operates three purpose-built motor service centres in Hong Kong, the total gross foot area of these centres is approximately 1.7mn sq ft, with the Kowloon Bay service centre reputed to be the largest in the world.

Traditionally, sales from the company represent approximately 25% of total new vehicle sales in the territory. However, after a substantial drop in car sales, especially in the non-luxury sector, earnings in 1995 suffered. In addition to the drop in car sales, the strong yen eroded profit margins during the early- and mid-1990s.

Motor Vehicles — PRC

In the PRC, DCH holds non-exclusive franchises for vehicles produced by Honda, Isuzu and Nissan. In addition, the company has established vehicle maintenance and spare part supply facilities in 10 major cities in the PRC. The largest importers of cars in the PRC are foreign-controlled joint ventures. Until 1 April 1994, foreign joint ventures in the PRC were exempt from import duties. Foreign vehicle sales in the PRC are currently more sluggish than sales in Hong Kong.

On the other hand, China's car makers were also hit by poor car sales in 1994 and 1995. The new rules requiring officials to drive locally-made vehicles boosted sales. But even among JVs producing import substitutes there have been difficulties in experiencing sales growth targets. Over the longer term, however, demand in the PRC is expected to outstrip supply and DCH will be perfectly placed with their extensive maintenance network to capitalise on this.

Food distribution and trading

DCH has developed into one of Hong Kong's leading importers of frozen meat and seafood. The group also distributes a wide range of specialty foods such as Norwegian salmon which they distribute to both restaurants and hotels. DCH has also established a retail network in Hong Kong with approximately 60 DCH Food Mart outlets, which stock frozen and specialty foods. With no major competitors in this niche DCH has been relatively successful in Hong Kong. In 1993 the group opened their first, and still only DCH Food Mart in the PRC.

DCH also acts as a distributor for electronic goods. Some of their largest brands include TEAC, Zanussi, Samsung, and Tannoy. Trading and distribution are expected to contribute to growth in the company's bottom line until the end of 1997.

Property

Investment property portfolio

CITIC's investment property portfolio (see table 6.1) predominantly consists of properties previously owned by Dah Chong Hong. The group is redeveloping a number of these sites, the largest of which is the old Quarry Bay motor service centre, located behind Swire Pacific's Taikoo Place, which is being developed into a 370,000 sq ft office tower, due for completion in the first half of 1997 when it is expected to contribute over HK$60mn. In 1998, its first full year, earnings are expected to reach HK$180mn.

CITIC's other major investment property will soon be one of Hong Kong's largest retail complexes. In a 50/50 joint venture with Swire Pacific, it is developing a 982,000 sq. ft. shopping centre above the interchange between the Mass Transit Railway and the Kowloon Canton Railway at Yau Yat Tsuen. The location was chosen as an extension of Swire Pacific's strategy of building in the vicinity of a large movement of people. The joint venture has already started negotiating with anchor tenants and the development is expected to be complete by the end of FY98. The first full year contribution from the project is expected be over HK$320mn.

Property provided a stable rental revenue of approximately HK$150mn in 1995. A 12.4% improvement to approximately HK$170mn was expected for 1996, and in 1997 when a contribution of over HK$600mn was expected.

Hong Kong Resort Company, 50% stake

CITIC acquired a 50% stake in Hong Kong Resort Company (HKRC) (not to be mistaken for the listed vehicle HKR International) in March 1994 for a consideration of HK$3.4bn. HKRC is primarily involved with property development projects in Discovery Bay. The development income of HKR in 1995 was secured through 1993/4 presales of residential units in Discovery Bay. Despite a lukewarm response to New World's Crestmont Villa in February 1995, the discounted selling prices for the launch of La Costa at an average of HK$3,850 per sq ft drew substantial buying interest with the initial 80 units oversubscribed almost 25 times. The strong demand led to the release of an additional 78 units which were also snapped up at an average of HK$3,950 per sq ft. Discovery Bay's future looks attractive — enhanced infrastructure, a low-density living environment and the possibility of a tunnel connection to the outside world should underpin property prices.

Table 6.1: CITIC Pacific property development schedule

Property	Usage	Attrib. GFA	Completion
Yee Lim Industrial Centre (CS&G)	Cold storage & godown	320,195	Existing
Kwai Fuk Road, Kwai Chung	Cold storage & godown	343,000	2H97
Taikoktsui Centre, 11–15 Kok Cheung St	Industrial	308,598	Existing
Belgravia, 57 South Bay Road	Residential	117,800	Existing
Honest Motors Building	Commercial	47,487	Existing
Wyler Centre	Industrial	393,488	Existing
Area 7, Tai Po	Residential	272,000	2H97
Wing Fong Road, Kwai Chung	Commercial	67,000	4Q96
Festival Walk–Yau Yat Tsuen	Office	115,285	2H98
Festival Walk–Yau Yat Tsuen	Commercial	951,789	2H98
Tamar Basin IL8822	Commercial	224,800	1H98
Westland Road, Quarry Bay	Commercial	370,000	2H97
Cheung Sha Wan	Industrial	250,000	2H98
Others in Japan	Residential & Commercial	60,069	Existing
TOTAL		**3,841,511**	
Development Properties			
7–17 Wing Fong Road, Kwai Chung (216 flats)	Residential	140,000	4Q96
Grand Court, Kadoorie Avenue	Residential	135,340	Existing

Likely government approval of additional developable land promises longer-term development earnings for HKRC. A formal application was made in December 1994 to the government to develop an additional 2,500 residential units comprising over 2.3mn sq ft. Based on the development schedule HKRC will contribute over HK$450mn in 1995 and over HK$480mn in 1996.

Consumer credit

Manhattan Card, 20% stake

The high-growth phase of Manhattan Card is over with and earnings projected to decelerate from 30% plus growth in recent years down to the high-teens by 1996. A number of negative factors are affecting future growth:

The rising cost of funds will hurt margins. While credit card lending is based on fixed rates (annualised at about 24%), funding is based on floating rates. The upturn in interest rates in late 1995–early 1996 inevitably hurt margins. Benefits from lower interest rates, which began in late 1996 was partly offset by growing competition in the consumer credit card business. Furthermore, the group recently resolved to issue floating rate certificates of deposit and securitise credit card receivables, which have both increased the average cost of funds.

Intense competition may also chip away market share. Major banks including Hang Seng Bank, OTB and Dah Sing Bank, are aggressively expanding their credit card business. In order to cope with increasing competition, Manhattan Card has launched aggressive marketing campaigns and incentive schemes, including waiving annual fees and free gift programmes. These programmes will reduce fee income on the one hand and increase operating costs on the other.

Recent statistics showed a drastic slowdown in retail sales in 1995–96, which in turn would lead to a slowdown in credit card receivable growth. In the first part of 1996, credit card receivables grew only 1–2% from the end of 1995.

Acquisitions and China infrastructure point the way forward
To maintain earnings growth, CITIC Pacific will have to rely on acquisitions, which are expected to carry an average rate of return of at least 15% (the ceiling for officially accepted returns in the PRC). Over the last two years the bulk of the acquisitions have been on the mainland where the group has focused on infrastructure. In late 1994 and late 1995, CITIC Pacific signed an agreement with local partners in Shanghai to acquire a 45% interest in a joint venture holding a 20-year exclusive franchise to operate the Nan Pu Bridge, Yang Pu Bridge and Da Pu Lu Tunnel in Shanghai. The facilities are operational and already are contributing to the bottom line. While the tunnels contributed only an estimated Rmb47.6mn in 1995, the terms of the joint venture allow CITIC to reap a guaranteed annual 15% return on their investment of US$300mn (HK$2.32bn) over the life of the project. Although this commitment does not have to be met by cash in the earlier years of the joint venture, the average return will be maintained and CITIC is expected to book an average return of HK$348.3mn every year until 2014.

CITIC Pacific also maintains a 50% interest in the Yan'an East Road Tunnel, where construction of an additional tube is proceeding as scheduled. The second tube was expected to be completed in mid-1996 at a projected cost of HK$1.63bn. Upon completion of the tunnel the group will have an interest in all of the facilities providing links between the old part of Shanghai Puxi, and the new town of Pudong across the Huang Pu River. It is expected the first contributions from the new tunnel will come in 1998. The existing tube of the Yan'an East Road Tunnel is already in operation and is generating an annual return of approximately HK$75mn. Returns from the project are also guaranteed at 15% during the franchise, which expires in 2024. With a 50% stake in the project, earnings from the tunnel will be recorded as a part of operating profit. Recently in a similar venture CITIC announced the acquisition of the Xu Li bridge in the PRC. Xu Li contributed US$15mn in 1996, rising to an expected US$30mn in 1997. At the end of 1995, infrastructure projects accounted for nearly 11% of the group's profit.

Power generation and a new push into PRC infrastructure

Ligang coal-fired power station

CITIC maintains a 56.3% interest in the Ligang coal fired power station in Jiangsu Province, PRC. The first two 350MW generators are in already in full operation and contributed an estimated HK$92.4mn in 1994. The second phase of Ligang, including another 2x350MW generators, is expected to be completed in 1998. The contract to build the plant was recently awarded to Westinghouse. Preliminary design work has now begun on phase 3, which is expected to house 2x800MW generators. CITIC will operate each of these facilities for 22 years.

Zhengzhou Xinli coal-fired power station

CITIC has a 50% interest in the Zhengzhou power plant which is in Henan Province, PRC. The first phase of the facility, comprising 2x200MW generators, is operational and the facility should have contributed about HK$24mn in 1994. Work on the second phase of the facility, adding another 200MW generator was completed in early 1996.

Pudong coal-fired power station

CITIC Pacific holds a 25% stake in the first phase of the Pudong Power Station in Shanghai. Construction of the 4x300MW facility has commenced and the first generator came on-line in March 1995. Two more generators came online during 1996, with the final generator being completed in 1997.

Kaifeng coal-fired power station

The group holds a 50% stake in the Kaifeng Power Station in Henan Province, PRC. Construction of the 1x125MW facility has commenced and the generator is expected to come online in early 1997. CITIC will operate the plant for a period of 20 years.

Industrial manufacturing facilities

CITIC has a controlling 55% interest in three manufacturing operations in the PRC:

- Jiangyin Xing Cheng Steel Works, which produces many grades of carbon and alloy steels. CITIC is committed to investing HK$420mn in the steel works, of which HK$231mn has already been contributed.
- Wuxi Tong Ling Cable, which manufactures plastic sheathed copper telephone wires and other cables for the telecommunications industry. The project will require a commitment of HK$88.8mn by CITIC of which HK$69mn has already been contributed
- Wuxi Honda Motors, which manufactures small to medium range motors for pumps and other industrial applications. This project requires a commitment of HK$59mn from CITIC of which HK$26.6mn has already been contributed.

Conclusion: does the counter deserve a PRC premium?

Valuation of this counter is complicated by the diversity of the businesses in which it is engaged. However, over the years it has become obvious that CITIC's nature as a "PRC concept stock" has enabled its share price to rocket to astonishing multiples. It has continued to trade at an estimated premium to NAV, and its new investments yield a 15% return. Even if CITIC has to rely on debt it will be successful in generating a positive return after paying off the debt. Investors expect that it will continually be able to secure attractive contracts that will enable growth. Any premium placed on CITIC is based on its continued ability to secure what investors perceive to be top-quality investments. Ultimately this depends on its ability to maintain superior *guanxi* on the mainland.

CHAPTER 7

Guangdong Enterprises and Guangdong Investment

Charles de Trenck

Guangdong Enterprises Holdings Limited (GEHL) was established in Hong Kong on 3 June 1980 (under the name of Guangdong Enterprises Ltd until 1986), just one year after the Open Door Policy was declared. In 1993, Guangdong Enterprises underwent a restructuring exercise for some of its subsidiaries and was converted into an unlisted public company. At the same time, additional second-tier holding companies were also established. Originally, the group was set up as a window for investment into Guangdong under the direction of the Guangdong provincial government. Having raised its profile as a holding company of a Hong Kong Hang Seng Index component in 1994, it must now be ready to undergo greater scrutiny from the public.

GEHL is the prototype of the complex development of Chinese companies. Since being established, GEHL has become a mini-conglomerate investing in every conceivable business in Guangdong. The group also has a few key investments outside Guangdong and property and trading ventures in France and the United States.

As a company, GEHL has a split personality. On the one hand, it reports to the provincial government of Guangdong, and on the other, it is attempting to establish a corporate image of a company that goes beyond a sovereign-risk backing. Both the parent and the listed company share the same chairman as well as a number of the same directors, many of whom had served in industry or with the Guangdong government. At the end of 1995, the group's total sales had grown to US$1.6b and total assets totaled US$3.5b. Because of high debt levels, net assets at the end of 1995 amounted to only US$647.0mn.

Guangdong Investment, the group's listed vehicle, was founded by way of a back-door entry in 1987 — one of the first of its kind for high-profile China-backed companies. In November 1994, it became a Hang Seng Index constituent (representing about 0.5% of the Index).

Mr He Keqin, 65, originally from Foshan, has been chairman of Guangdong Investment since its inception. He also was named chairman of the group in 1992, after being deputy general manager during 1981–85 and general manager during 1985–92. Mr He began his career in the handicraft industry of Foshan (1949–66) and later worked in the northern Guangdong city of Shaoguan (1967–80), serving first at Shaoguan Steel, and later in a fertilizer company.

In order to spruce up its image in early 1997 following a lacklustre group performance during the mid-1990s, the listed company announced the arrival of Herbert Hui as the new managing director of Guangdong Investment. The appointment of Mr Hui, the former head of the Hong Kong Stock Exchange's listing division, was interpreted by investors as an attempt by the listed company to begin a new phase of acquisitions and corporate transactions.

This chapter will explore some of the issues involved in the parent-listed vehicle relationship and will consider the viability of some of the financing structures set into motion by the group. Guangdong Enterprises has become a master builder of complex conglomerate structures.

Looking at the issues raised from a more macro-economic perspective, readers will want to weigh Guangdong Enterprises' corporate activities against the prospects for Guangdong province's slowing growth relative to both its own record and to the national average. Also relevant to the conclusions drawn will be the issues of the downgrading of corporate debt and the ensuing higher cost of capital for the group. However, the cost of capital issue will also rise as a result of a potential higher cost of capital in Hong Kong, and therefore also in Guangdong, following the 1997 handover, as argued in the introductory chapter.

The Guangdong economic miracle

Guangdong has clearly created its own economic centre of gravity in China. It has been an economic powerhouse since the Open Door Policy took root as well as since Hong Kong entrepreneurs decided to move their manufacturing operations out of Hong Kong — much of it into Guangdong. Growth has been focused along the Pearl River Delta, home to some 25mn people out of Guangdong's total population of 67.8mn people in 1995. Most measures of economic activity put the province at the head of the growth pack in China. Its 1995 GDP per capita was Rmb7,937, 67% higher than the national average and the highest among provinces (excluding Shanghai and Beijing). Although Guangdong represented under 10% of China's GDP in 1995, it accounted for 40% of total exports and 38% of total imports.

In addition to importing Hong Kong's industrial capacity throughout the 1980s, relaxation of China's formerly unforgiving household registration system in the province has allowed the type of migration needed to staff new factories in southern Guangdong. Shenzhen, which has become an economic area of over 3.5mn people within 15 years, and which is by far and away the largest and most successful of the SEZs, would not have been possible without a complete overhaul of the household registration system, which, prior to economic reforms in the 1980s, restricted freedom of movement within China. Shenzhen owes much of its dynamism to migration patterns. Although there are only 1mn registered permanent residents of Shenzhen City, which comprises surrounding counties, about 2.6mn are registered as temporary residents and it is estimated that another million are part of the floating population.

Analysis of data from a 1990 census put the rate of immigration into Guangdong at over 1.1mn persons per year. Intra-Guangdong migration was twice as high. Since then these figures have only increased. Moreover, much immigration into Guangdong is liable to be under-counted as a result of the waves of migrant labourers that flow into Guangdong seeking short-term employment every year, with a large proportion flowing back out after a stint in a factory. One has only to board a local train from Guangzhou to Shenzhen, or take a tour of the Guangzhou train station, to realise that Guangdong's migrant labour force is enormous. The largest flows of migrant labour usually are experienced just before and just after the Chinese New Year. As a result of slowing economic growth in 1997, the rate of migration into Guangdong is expected to be flat during 1997. However, the return of Hong Kong to Chinese rule in July 1997 may also result in a redistribution of migration patterns, with Pearl River Delta areas receiving an initial population inflow from economic migrants seeking to live the Hong Kong dream. The most likely outcome of the migration pattern may very well be a jump in inflows of workers to Shenzhen and other neighbouring regions, despite government attempts to limit them.

Is a fall from grace around the corner?

Guangdong's economic growth has outperformed that of China since reforms began, turning in an average GDP growth rate of 17.8% per year between 1986 and 1995 — a 6.7% premium to the national GDP growth average for the same period. These figures are based on data released by authorities in autumn 1996.

Guangdong is likely to continue to do well through to the end of the century, partly because it will continue to attract migrants from other provinces who are willing to work for less to achieve their bit of the Guangdong economic miracle. However, the extent to which its growth exceeds the national average is likely to slow. With manufacturing costs in the Pearl River Delta continuing to spiral upwards, and with Beijing likely to curtail tax and other incentives in China's coastal regions, Guangdong will more likely see its growth rate settle at parity or just the long-term 9% GDP growth potential China is capable of delivering.

Contrasts between the economies of Guangdong and China

7.1: Guangdong and China GDP growth

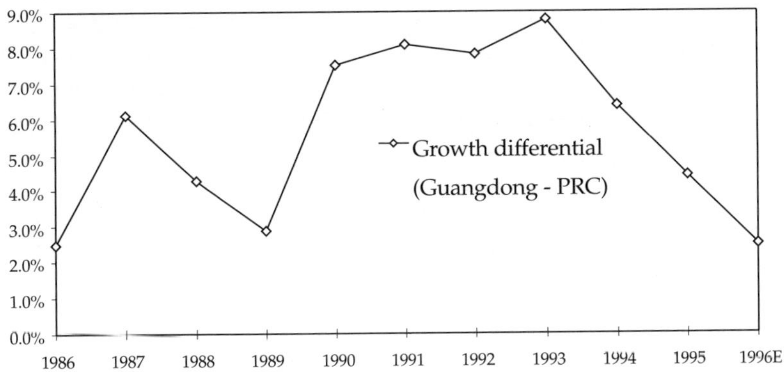

Source: Guangdong Statistical Yearbook 1996

7.2: Guangdong and China export growth

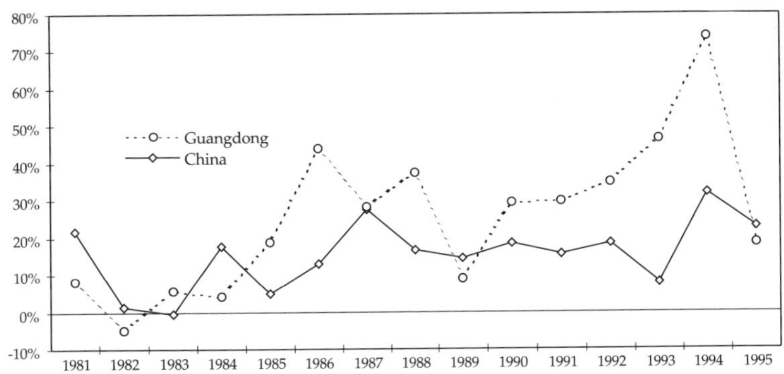

Differences between the parent and the listed flagship

One of the first items noticed by investors and analysts of state-backed companies was the lack of division between governmental goals and corporate observance of the bottom line. This is the crucial point that sets China's own brand of capitalism apart from that in most developed economies. This is not to say that Chinese companies do not seek to generate profits from their assets, but that, invariably, a substantial portion of assets just do not perform well.

Since the credit rating downgrades during 1994–95, and given growing doubts as to what exactly sovereign backing really means for a Chinese firm, it is a matter of urgency that the group progress beyond a sovereign-risk rating following Beijing's continued cutbacks in financial support for companies in Guangdong. It is also a matter of importance that Guangdong Investment develop its own separate identity and track record. Behind this development would lie the formation of an independent investment strategy that would no longer rely on acquisitions from the parent.

7.3: Guangdong Enterprises group chart

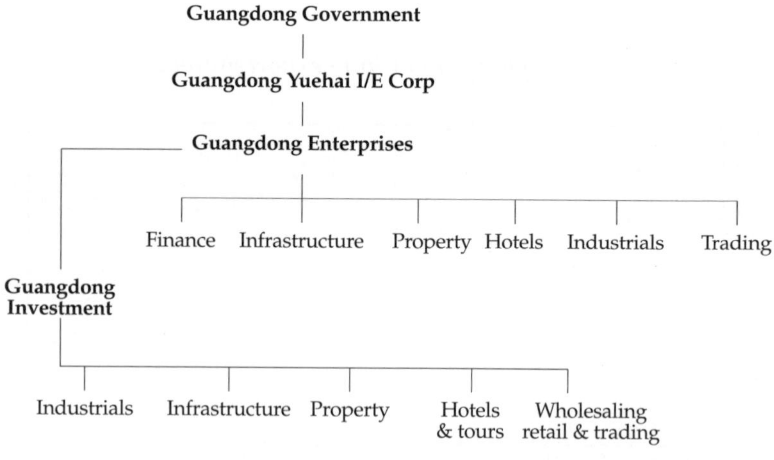

Over the last decade and a half, Guangdong Enterprises has grown into a sprawling agglomeration of industrial enterprises, infrastructure projects, hotels and property investments. The basic structure of the listed company is similar to that of the parent. The main difference is that the best of these companies are injected into the listed vehicle under complex transactions that often allow the listed company to consolidate non-controlling interests in companies that are ultimately controlled by the holding (see figure 7.3, Guangdong Enterprises group chart, and table 7.1, GEHL Major subsidiaries, investments and projects).

The major division investors latch on to is that of the holding company, which has a hand in nearly every industry, and the listed company, which shows the face of an organised conglomerate to the investing public. Table 7.1 summarises the parent's major assets and investments. A few years ago the list was longer, but a number of key subsidiaries, including a brewery, hotels and properties, have been injected into the listed company, which is classified as an associate on the books of the parent.

The listed vehicle: almost picture-perfect

The listed company is a well-groomed, neatly compartmentalised company, complete with defined strategic investment sectors designed to please investors. Also designed to please is a pledge from management to produce strong year-on-year earnings per share growth, not an easy task for Chinese companies. In 1994, the management would typically tell investors that target earnings per share growth was 20% per year. Guangdong Investment delivered about 15% earnings per share growth in 1994 and about 8% in 1995, and has done well enough to satisfy institutional investors during a difficult period for earnings growth from China-related counters. But this growth was not achieved without substantial last-minute assistance from the parent, as will be explained below.

GDI's earnings growth in 1994 and 1995 was produced through well-timed acquisitions of growing subsidiaries held by the parent, with one notable exception being the acquisition of a power generation investment in the northern Guangdong city of Shaoguan from the Guangdong Bureau of Power (and therefore not an acquisition from a related party). The Shaoguan 300MW

Table 7.1: ***GEHL major subsidiaries, investments & projects*** *(as of December 1995)*

Stake	*Manfacturing*	**BV 1994** (US$mn)	**BV 1995** (US$mn)	**change**
60%	Changshan Cement	19.4	22.5	16%
70%	Zhong Yue Tin Plate	41.5	25.2	-39.3%
60%	Guangdong Dragon Timber	6.5	25.5	292.3%
75%	Jiang Yin Yue Yang Auto Air	4.7	16.0	240.4%
60%	Foshan Guangdong Automotive	13.0	8.5	-34.6%
40%	Yellow Dragon Food	15.5	13.4	-13.5%
100%	Universal Garment	5.7	6.0	5.3%
90%	Mansfield Garment	6.2	6.4	3.2%
13%	Guangzhou Iron & Steel	50.0	26.2	-47.6%
5%	Shaoguan Iron & Steel	11.9	16.9	42.0%
40%	Heshan Haishan Spandex Factory	6.1	5.4	-11.5%
80%	Dongguan Yuelin Furniture	5.8	18.9	225.9%
40%	Zhaoqing Micro Fiber	6.9	8.9	29.0%
35%	Xinhui Honda Decorative Textiles	0	6.5	na
	Total	**193.2**	**206.3**	**6.8%**
	Infrastructure investments			
	Guangdong (Panyu) Petrochemical			
	Guangzhou–Zhuhai Expressway			
	Panyu Bridge			
	Shenzhen Airport–Heao Highway			
	Hotel operations	**Rooms**	**City**	
	Yuehai Centre	51	Guangzhou	
	Guangdong Hotel	309	Zhuhai	
	Guangdong Resort (50%)	85	Panyu	
	Guangdong Regency Hotel	400	Beijing	
	Regina Hotel	315	Bangkok	
	Seaview Hotel (10%)	160	Pattaya	
	Guangdong Hotel (33%)	181	Paris	

plant, acquired in mid-1994, has proven to be one of the most successful arm's-length transactions of the listed company.

The asset shuffle approach to earnings growth
Another interpretation of recent earnings growth is that it was generated through asset shuffling amongst subsidiaries of the holding and the listed company. In 1994 and 1995, the group initiated a new phase of this, with a two-step spin-off process which involved, first, both an injection and a listing of the food trading subsidiary, Guangnan Hang, and, second, the resale of the injected portion back to the parent. This particular transaction will be discussed in detail below. Asset shuffling to generate non-recurring profits is, of course, considered a lower-quality source of earnings.

Financial structure of the parent
If the listed company is perceived as an organised and compartmentalised company, the holding company is quite the opposite. As a result of multiple holdings of a hodge-podge of investments and subsidiaries across Guangdong, GEHL maintains a low profit margin before accounting for exceptional items. Moreover, because the parent is away from the prying eyes of the investing public, and is backed by Guangdong province, debt levels (excluding minority interests as liabilities) were left to approach 3.2x the 1995 equity base, or 3.7x the equity base when including minority interests as liabilities. These levels were about eight times higher than the listed vehicle's levels.

Operating profit before interest in 1995 was enough to pay the heavy interest burden and leave about an equal amount to add to contributions from associates, which for the most part was from Guangdong Investment. The measure used to evaluate a firm's ability to service its debt, interest cover, was about 1.9x. For an ongoing concern the interest cover would be considered relatively weak, but compared to groups similar to Guangdong Enterprises, the debt/equity and interest cover measures, among other ratios, are considered in line with the norm. A glance at the consolidated cash flow reveals that cash outflow from operating activities was negative in both 1994 (negative HK$549.2mn) and 1995 (negative

HK$661.7mn), with the main reasons being a very substantial deterioration in the group's receivables and inventories.

About the only difference between the group and other state-backed companies is the greater degree of financial engineering the group is able to carry off. Figures 7.4 and 7.5 illustrate the different profitability levels between the holding company and the listed company.

7.4: GE & GI operating profit margins

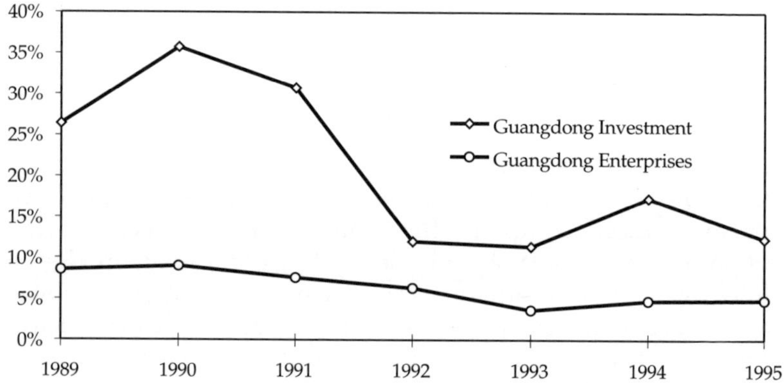

7.5: GE & GI net profit margins

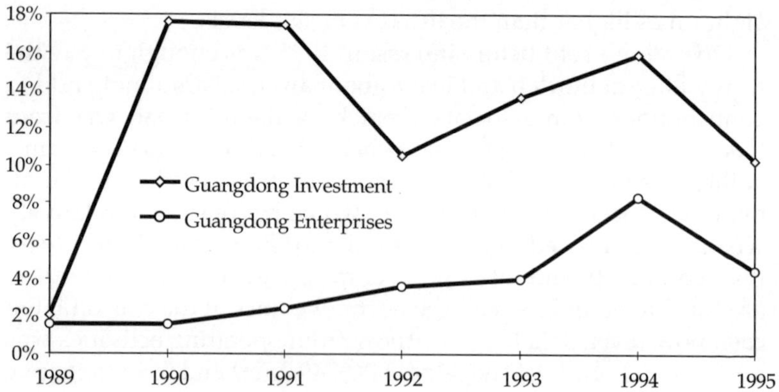

What happened to 1992's assets?

In 1993, the group revised downward its net assets recorded in 1992 by 42%. One principal qualification listed by the auditor in the 1992 accounts read: "We have been unable to satisfy ourselves as to the carrying value of certain interests in subsidiary and associated companies, the audited financial statements of which have not been made available for our inspection. Accordingly, a few of the subsidiaries and all associated companies have not been consolidated in the group financial statements." When GEHL made available an offering circular to international investors in June 1994 during a debt-raising exercise for a US$150mn Floating Rate Note (FRN), the 1992 accounts had been completely restated and the net assets (assets minus liabilities) of the company as at end 1992 had been reduced by 42% as compared with the presentation the preceding year. The main differences in the accounts was the recalculation of the net assets of most associates and some subsidiaries. Whereas in 1992 information on associates had apparently omitted many of their liabilities, the 1993 accounts reflected the reduction in the net asset values of the associates as a result of the inclusion of additional liabilities.

Not surprisingly, the pricing on the FRN issue was six-month LIBOR + 2%, nearly 100 basis points higher than the company had been used to paying up to this issue. Why did Western banks not ask for a higher return for their higher risk loans earlier? The answer may very well be that some banks had obviously overlooked the level of risk involved with the group from the beginning. The issue is similar to the Moody's downgrading of GITIC and Guangdong Enterprises in 1995: Shouldn't the downgrades have been made a few years earlier, when the conglomerate embarked on its borrowing campaigns with foreign institutions? As it turned out, Moody's had raised the ratings of a few Chinese firms during the early 1990s, only to lower them two years later. Guangdong Enterprises was one of those whose credit rating was lowered.

The increased cost of borrowing for Guangdong Enterprises in 1994, and to a lesser extent in 1995, was also tied to concerns over China's economic stability during the first part of its new austerity programme, and to concerns over Deng Xiaoping's failing health.

As these concerns gradually receded in 1996, Guangdong Enterprises' cost of capital fell back as well. At the same time, however, many banks were again courting Hong Kong–based companies after a period of uncertainty over lending past the 1997 handover. To be noted is that the Guangdong Enterprises group of companies was in 1996 still paying 30–50 basis points more for its capital than it had paid in the early 1990s. Using data supplied by IFR Securities Data, figure 7.6 reconstitutes the movement in the spread above LIBOR or HIBOR group companies have paid since 1990. All-in costs are also calculated by taking management fees charged by lenders divided by the estimated average life of the loans and added to the loan spread.

7.6: Guangdong Enterprises' cost of debt

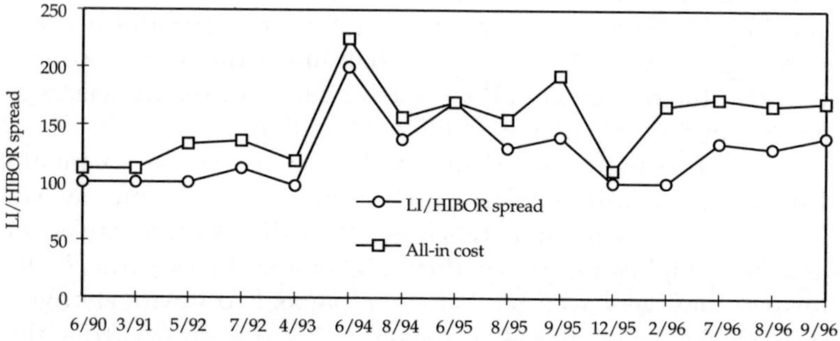

Source: IFR Securities Database

How to give analysts a migraine

The complexity of transactions within the group has reached dizzying heights. Equity analysts covering the listed company are left with endless strings of formulae on monstrously large spreadsheets incorporating dozens of subsidiaries and investments. Within the course of an accounting year, these subsidiaries can appear and disappear, and grow and shrink capriciously. The forecasting of items such as minority interests is turning into more of a black art than calculation.

Other items facing credit analysts are the shifting of GEHL's collateral. For instance, pledges of shares held in Guangdong Investment from specific subsidiaries can be used for raising debt for the holding company. In the early 1990s, 100% held subsidiaries such as Wincall Investment, Jingmei Travel and Guangdong Finance would shift the stakes they held in Guangdong Investment amongst themselves. At the same time, some of the funds borrowed from the subsidiaries were backed by the pledge of shares in Guangdong Investment held by these subsidiaries. Theoretically, therefore, one of the jobs of the banker loaning the funds was to track these changes to ensure that the subsidiaries were not under-collateralised at any one point in time. However, since Guangdong Enterprises has traditionally been viewed as supported by the provincial government, bankers have always thought that GEHL would be supported by it in the case of any corporate difficulty.

For equity analysts, the purpose of an analysis of the listed company is, of course, to forecast future earnings growth. In order to deliver the growth demanded by investors, the group has done what is necessary to achieve reasonable earnings growth for the listed vehicle, even if it means injecting the parent's strongest cash cow (Guangnan) during the last two months of the year and finding a way to book an exceptional from it. To the listed company's credit, it has taken pity on the plight of analysts by answering many of their queries on a number of complicated issues involving subsidiaries, with one major exception being the company's tours division.

Guangdong Investment's blind spot: the hotel and tours division

The hotel and tours division has traditionally shied away from disclosing its operating profit breakdown. It only supplies an agglomerated contribution to earnings, despite its managing a multitude of dissimilar operations, including hotels, tour groups and a trading operation for appliances. Management acknowledges the existence of the trading division within the tours company only grudgingly. It hardly ever provides clear information on the division to inquiring analysts and investors, and it does not describe the operation in its annual report.

Still with regards to the hotel and tours division, it has been mentioned more than once that some profits of the division during the early 1990s had come from the trading of currencies, and that the operation was closed down following high-profile scandals within CITIC Shanghai and other China-backed groups. When it has discussed the issue at all, GDI has indicated that non-core earnings from the division were no longer significant after 1993. This development may have explained why the 1994 contribution from the hotel and tours division was flat when compared to 1993, despite an injection of hotels from the group that increased the average number of rooms by over 50% during the year. The cost to investors in April 1994 for enlarging the hotel and tours division was HK$819.3mn for stakes in two hotels owned by the parent, which was financed through the issue of 187.9mn new shares. A more recent interview with the company in late 1996 revealed that the hotel and tours division expected a rebound in contribution from the trading of appliances in 1996, indicating that, after a lull in appliances trading from the low levels in 1994 and 1995, the division had decided that concentrating part of its energies in trading was more worth its while than focusing on its core hotel and tour operations.

A brief look at the listed company's cash flow statement

Despite China's 1994–95 recessionary environment, the group generated profits by swapping assets and intra-group transactions. But a profit from intra-group sales does not mean that a contribution is made to cash coming into the company's coffers, since a number of intra-group accounts can be adjusted to account for such asset swaps. The place to find all the answers is the cash flow statement, which quite often tells a very different story than the profit and loss statement.

At the operating cash flow level, GDI in 1994 reversed a net outflow from operating activities in 1993 with a HK$711.7mn net cash inflow. This figure meant that after accounting for intra-group cash flows and changes in inventory and accounts receivable and payable, and after adding back GDI's HK$106.6mn depreciation charges, operating cash flow was approximately in line with the P&L's operating profit plus the depreciation charge. During the previous accounting year, the same exercise yielded a cash outflow of HK$33mn, or some HK$423mn less than the P&L's operating profit.

A look further down the cash flow statement, however, reveals that cash flow after investing but before financing was negative in both years. The 1994 statement revealed a HK$662.6mn deficit, up from 1993's HK$2.3bn deficit. This was due to acquisitions of new investments and outlays for development of properties. Naturally, funds were raised to pay for the outlays. The question which must be asked on the basis of looking back on operations in 1995 and 1996, is whether new acquisitions and investments performed in line with expectations?

The 1995 cash flow statement revealed a more worrisome deterioration in cash flow at the operating level, indicating that investments of past years were not returning as much as expected. Net cash flow from operating activities was HK$403.0 mn in 1995, or HK$502.5mn less than operating profit. Much of the shortfall was made up by increases in inventory and accounts receivable. Purchases of new assets led the company to register a net deficit of HK$1.4bn in cash flow after investing but before financing. The shortfall was again matched by raising new funds. The question will again have to be asked of the 1996 statements: were funds raised put to good use?

It could be argued that negative cash flows before financing are likely to be a standard feature for red chip cash flow statements, since it is in their nature to grow through acquisitions and that these acquisitions are funded through share placements and bank loans. However, it is notable that during 1995 the book value of Guangdong Investment grew only from HK$5.1bn to HK$5.6bn and that the book value per share actually decreased from HK$2.84 to HK$2.61 after accounting for dilution from new shares issued during the year.

It is upon the cash flow statement that long-term growth issues will be decided. Theoretically, the practice of supporting profits at the expense of ignoring cash flow can continue for quite some time. GDI simply needs to issue new shares and borrow more money for new assets, and in the process it can continue to raise funds needed for existing operations. But what if investors no longer find the parent's remaining assets or other potential acquisitions as attractive as they found past acquisitions? Over the long term, Guangdong Investment clearly needs to focus on managing its existing investments.

A brief history of acquisitions from the parent

In order to continue to appeal to investors, a key strategy open to Guangdong Investment is to allow equity investors access to the parent's stronger subsidiaries, if there are any left. The history of Guangdong Investment has been one long list of acquisitions from the parent. There is of course, nothing wrong with acquiring assets from the parent. What counts is that the price is fair and that an injection contributes positively to earnings growth. And as pointed out, some acquisitions are from other Guangdong province government entities, and are not classified as related-party transactions. One could argue, therefore, that the listed company does not depend on the parent alone for new assets. Yet, a closer analysis reveals that the great majority of star acquisitions have been from the parent. As the record stands, acquisitions have by and large benefited investors through 1995, and the listed company's share price has performed with satisfaction. There are, however, a number of issues to pursue with these acquisitions, some of which will be covered below. Table 7.2 provides details of major corporate transactions since the company's inception.

The first point to note is that control of assets that were originally under the parent remains with the parent, since GEHL calls all the shots for Guangdong Investment through what has traditionally been a 43–46% stake in the listed company. Effective control is maintained despite the fact that less than 50% of shares are controlled by the parent. The stake is classified as an associate in the GEHL accounts. In September 1996, the group placed 80mn shares to investors, and brought its stake in its listed vehicle below 40%.

First steps

Between July 1988, when the company changed its name to Guangdong Investment and directly identified itself with its parent, and December 1991, Guangdong Investment was essentially a property company. In December 1991, GDI sprang to life

Table 7.2: Guangdong Investment corporate history

Corporate History, Major fund raising & acquisitions

(values in HK$ mn equivalent)

		Funds raised	Funds spent
Jan 87	Guangdong Enterprises acquires a 63.5% stake in Union Globe Development		
Jul 88	Name change to Guangdong Investment Ltd		
Jan 91	Rights issue of 73.2mn shares at HK$0.55	40.2	
Jun 91	Acquisition of Cameron Centre for HK$156mn		156.0
Nov 91	Acquires a 20% stake in Citybus for HK$50mn		50.0
Dec 91	460mn new shares issued at HK$1.20 and 1 for 5 12/94 warrants issued at HK$1.30	765.0	
Dec 91	Acquisitions of Guangdong Tour ($370mn), 44.2% stake in Guangzhou Malt ($62mn), 4.1m sq ft Panyu site ($66.3mn)		498.3
Jun 92	540mn new shares issued at HK$3.00	1,620.0	
Jun 92	Acquisitions of 24.5% of Shenzhen Brewery, 70% stake in Guangdong Hotel and Irving Court, Cao Yang Village and a Guangzhou Property, and 80% of Full Arts		780.0
Dec 92	Aquired 60.8% of Weili Washing Machines for HK$297mn		297.0
Mar 93	JV with Swank for Guangdong retailing		24.0
Jul 93	Acquires 5% stake in CIL		14.4
Sep 93	Guangdong Corp, whose major stake is Full Arts, is spun-off in Australia (funds go direct to Full Arts)		
Sep 93	US$102mn 4.5% convertible bond issued, due Oct 1998 and convertible into shares priced at HK$3.84	787.4	
Sep 93	Acquires passive 95% stake in Zhongshan Power's 50MW plant		220.8
Sep 93	Invests in Shiqi section of Guangzhou–Zhuhai highway		100.0
Dec 93	Shenzhen Brewery stake is raised to 64.5% (implied acquisition P/E is 9x)		129.8
Apr 94	Issue of 187.9mn new shares at HK$4.36 per share	819.3	
Apr 94	Acquisition of Wharney and Guangdong hotels from the parent		819.3

Table 7.2: Guangdong Investment corporate history

	Corporate History, Major fund raising & acquisitions (*values in HK$ mn equivalent*)	Funds raised	Funds spent
May 94	Stake in Guangdong Corp (Full Arts) is increased by 10%		18.6
Jun 94	45.9% stake in 300MW Shaoguan Power announced (completed August), HK$550mn		550.0
Aug 94	New York ADRs established		
Aug 94	124mn and 37.5mn new shares issued at HK$4.90 and HK$4.96, respectively	793.6	
Aug 94	Acquisition of 75.6% stake in Nanhai Tannery, Hainan (on P/E of 5.3x guaranteed 1994 profits)		186.0
Nov 94	Acquisition of 34.7% stake in Guangnan Hang (26% after spin-off in Hong Kong) from Guangdong Enterprises (on P/E of 7.5x)		111.0
Jun 95	Buys a 56% stake in Nanfang Dept store for HK$170mn		170.0
Nov 95	Disposal of stake in Guangnan for HK$343.5mn	343.5	
Nov 95	Disposal of 25.6% stake in Weili Group for HK$85mn, (about 28.5% loss on original invst)	85.0	
Apr 96	Commits HK$109.8mn (US$14.2mn) to an effective 12.5% stake in 2x125MW Meixian generators, through a 49% stake in GD Power		109.8
May 96	Completed early conversion of its Oct 1998 US$102mn CB by 3 May, resulting in 205.4mn new share issuance during 5 Dec 95–3 May 96		
Jun 96	Acquisition of remaining 24.4% stake of Nanhai Tannery & Leather for HK$88.2 mn		277.0
Aug 96	Places 80mn shares at HK$5.22	417.6	
Aug 96	Sells its 20% stake in Citybus for HK$98mn	98.0	
Sep 96	Acquires 50% stake in Guangzhou–Zhuhai expressway JV holding 40% (effective 20%; NWI equal share) for HK$112mn		112.0
Sep 96	Buys for HK$1.2bn Sheung Wan 183,229 sq ft, 27F Grade B building. Issues 96mn new shares at HK$5.32	510.7	1,200
	TOTALS	**6,280.3**	**5,824.0**

with the issue of new warrants and shares raising HK$765mn. With the money, it entered into agreements with its parent to acquire stakes in GEHL's tour company, a malt plant and a piece of property in Panyu outside Guangzhou for a little less than HK$500mn. A few months later, in June 1992, GDI went back to the market to raise HK$1.62bn for more purchases from its parent, this time for a stake in a Shenzhen Brewery, a curtain wall specialist and some hotels and properties. The funds invested were again close to half the amount raised, with the balance going for working capital.

"Working capital", technically funds on hand to carry out daily operations of the company, is quite often a worrisome category during fund raising because the investor is never quite sure where the funds will be spent — particularly if there is too much of it.

Turning the simple into the complex

A complex trail could be found with one quick look into one of the 1992 acquisitions, that of an 80% stake in the curtain wall company, Full Arts, for HK$60.4mn. The same company was in September 1993 itself also bundled into a separate investment in Australia, Guangdong Corp, while remaining under the control of Guangdong Investment (and therefore Guangdong Enterprises).

The Full Arts acquisition trail would lead the curious to a number of offshore BVI companies, where both the acquiring and acquired companies swapped debt, cash and assets at valuations that will never be known to the investors who witnessed only the final HK$60.4mn acquisition by the listed company. No less than four group companies (one from the parent and three from the listed company) were used to complete the acquisition. The question here would be, what was the value of the company to be injected before it began its journey offshore?

Such a transaction was by no means out of the ordinary, as a number of other Hong Kong companies engage in the same practice. But the deal's complexity cannot but leave unanswered questions as to why such a small acquisition required so much complexity.

The infrastructure kick

In the fall of 1993, GDI shifted gears and moved to expand its line of business. First it raised funds through a US$102mn convertible bond issue (redeemed early in May 1996), which was well received by international investors. Flush with new funds, the company invested HK$220.8mn in a 50MW power station in Zhongshan, HK$100.8mn in a section of the Guangzhou-Zhuhai Expressway, and HK$129.8mn in upping its stake in Shenzhen Brewery to 64.5% before the end of the year, and an unspecified amount toward increasing GDI's stake in the Tianhe shopping complex. Not more than HK$336.8mn was left for Tianhe and the unused portion. Another planned investment in a larger 400MW plant was left for the following June and August, despite the fact that a letter of intent had been signed just prior to the convertible and that the convertible bond prospectus mentioned that the current net proceeds would help contribute to part of the acquisition. One could infer that funds were insufficient to complete such a large acquisition, which totaled HK$550mn for a 46% stake in 300MW.

To complete the acquisition another cash call was needed, and in August 1994, the same month the 300MW power plant was completed, the company made two share placements to raise HK$793.6mn. An additional acquisition of a stake in 100MW of power generation at Shaoguan D was never completed. The acquisitions that followed, and that supposedly called for the fund raising exercise, totaled HK$297mn. The money spent was put to good use, since a 75.6% stake in a high-growth leather tannery and an effective 26% stake (after listing) in the then soon-to-be-listed Guangnan Holdings were taken in the fall of 1994. But the fact remained that substantial amounts, in this case a balance of HK$496.6mn, were being set aside for the working capital and, arguably, cost over-runs, of other operations.

A quieter 1995

Following these acquisitions, GDI settled into a relatively quiet 1995. Asian markets were weak and there were no new corporate transactions that could be envisaged. Moreover, perhaps for the first time, GDI was faced with the task of growing its own assets. Expansion of brewing and malting operations went ahead as scheduled, with 100,000 tonnes of additional capacity being added at both Shenzhen Brewery and Guangzhou Malt. The Guangzhou Malt expansion, though sharing the same production area, was named Yangcheng Malting for the purposes of creating a new corporate entity that could qualify for the standard tax breaks enjoyed by start-up operations in China. With the standard corporate tax in China at 33%, most firms have learned to be as tax efficient as possible.

One rather substantial hiccough was the slower than expected opening of a new 1.7mn sq ft shopping centre in Guangzhou, Tianhe Mall, in the new growth district of Tianhe. There, the company was running about nine months late in completing construction and was having trouble finding anchor tenants. As it turned out, the first anchor tenant was Nanfang Department Store, a company in which it acquired a 56% stake in 1995. Another problem was that the US$200mn project, now 51% owned by GDI, had already spent about US$35–40mn on building the foundations for planned office and hotel towers (as part of the next phase). But the property market in the Tianhe district appeared headed for an over-supply situation and the plans had to be shelved.

The last few months of 1995

The company has traditionally waited until the end of the financial year to complete its housekeeping. And so, in the last two months of 1995, Guangdong Investment initiated a round of adjustments in its assets to free up additional funds for existing expansion plans and to help it adjust its target profit for the financial year. The stake in Guangnan Holdings, which had been acquired one year earlier for the long term, was now sold back to the parent. At the same time, a controlling stake in Weili Washing Machine was brought back down to that of an associate. GDI tried for the better part of two years to spin-off its stake in Weili, but it was too apparent that profits were drying up for this manufacturer of small-sized washing machines. By mid-1995, operating margins had shrunk from just above an estimated 10% to below 5% within a 12 month period. With no buyers in sight in November, management reduced its stake in Weili from 60.8% to 36.5%.

The case of Guangnan

In late 1994, GEHL sold a part of its food trading subsidiary, Guangnan Holdings, to equity investors and its listed vehicle. Because it was the flagship and because GDI ended up selling its effective 26% stake back to the parent, the acquisition and disposal merit a closer analysis.

From the perspective of the listed company, the purchase was meant to add a new earnings-enhancing company to Guangdong Investment. It was claimed that the investment would be held long term. Exactly one year later, Guangdong Investment resold its stake back to the parent, generating a gain on disposal of about HK$132mn. The profit was possible after more than a tripling in the share price of the subsidiary being traded between holding and listed vehicle. The November 1994 IPO of Guangnan Holdings was priced at HK$1.03. More than a year later, the share price traded above HK$5, and by early 1997 the shares traded at the HK$10 level.

One standard (and perfectly logical) strategy is to hold a profitable investment until the end of the year such that the profits can contribute to operating profits. When the investment is disposed of toward the end of the financial year, the company gains both the contribution for the year and the gain on the disposal. In this case, the Guangnan sale was used to both contribute to the bottom line and to help provide a sorely needed exceptional gain to boost earnings beyond the level of the previous year.

Guangnan's original spin-off represented a classical Guangdong Enterprises manoeuvre. It was designed with the usual complexity, with ultimate control held by the parent, but with Guangdong Investment still able to book its stake in Guangnan Holdings as a subsidiary rather than as an associate. This is because Guangnan was held by Guangdong Enterprises through three separate vehicles, while Guangdong Investment, itself one of the vehicles, controlled only one intermediary holding company, Guangnan International, as outlined in the shareholding structure in figures 7.7 and 7.8.

Guangnan holding structure

7.7: After sale to public and GDI

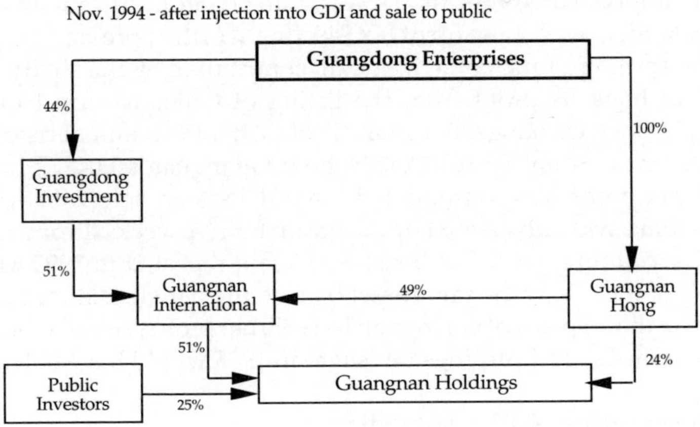

7.8: After partial resale back to parent

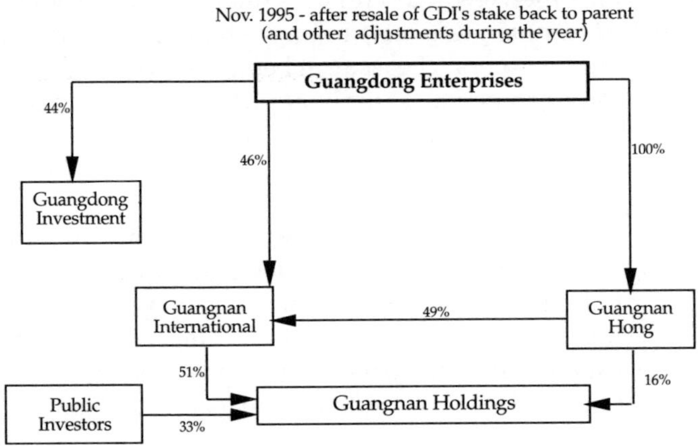

The great advantage of injecting Guangnan into the listed company was that it was able to book a desperately needed year-end earnings boost in 1994 and 1995. Without Guangnan, GDI wouldn't have had a hope of earning more than HK$400mn in 1994, a number it had to reach if it was to maintain the confidence of institutional investors. Its HK$437.2mn net profit attributable to shareholders was made up of HK$49.1mn worth of pre-tax exceptional earnings, much of it, if not all, contributed by the ability of GDI to book its profit from the listing of Guangnan on Hong Kong's stock exchange. An analysis of GDI's 1994 annual report, however, does not reveal exactly how Guangnan's HK$73.1mn 1994 net profit was consolidated into GDI's own net profit. The subsidiary was only owned by the group for five weeks during the 1994 accounting year. The boost was again repeated in 1995 as a result of the sale of the same asset back to the parent. Without the gain on the disposal of Guangnan in 1995, net profit growth would have been flat and earnings per share in 1995 would have fallen.

A closer look at GEHL subsidiaries

Since the group's mission is to develop industries in Guangdong, it has taken stakes in a variety of enterprises across the province. The more profitable investments are later injected into the listed vehicle. The group not only faces the issue of having to rationalise its diverse operations and investments, it also has to contend with a multitude of local governments. These local authorities can sometimes take the view that GEHL is the wealthy outsider and give it almost as much difficulty in improving operations as that faced by foreign partners. The issue of being considered a wealthy outside investor can be particularly applicable when acquisition prices are discussed amongst buyer and seller.

Guangdong Capital Holdings

The 100% controlled subsidiary, known as Wincall Investment until 1993, was created in 1986 as one of Guangdong Enterprises' principal funding vehicles. In 1993, the subsidiary underwent a face-lift designed to lead GEHL into establishing a profit centre in corporate finance and securities. One principal subsidiary, Guangdong Securities, now holds two seats on the Hong Kong

Stock Exchange and trades actively in securities, and conducts investment banking activities relating to IPOs for Guangdong province companies and Guangdong Enterprises' related share offerings (Guangnan Holdings). Other activities include fund management and consulting.

Industrial operations

GEHL has increased its exposure to over 80 industrial projects after initiating its first industrial investments during the mid-1980s. Major investments range from steel and cement plants to automobile production. The higher growth operations, Shenzhen Brewery, Guangzhou Malt and Nanhai Tannery, were all injected into the listed company in 1993 and 1994. Its largest remaining investment in its industrial portfolio in 1994 was a 28% stake in Guangzhou Iron & Steel valued at US$50mn, which was subsequently sold down in 1995 to a 12.6% stake.

Guangzhou Iron & Steel, one of Guangdong's leading steel producers, was established as an equity JV in 1988 between GEHL and a Guangzhou government-owned steel plant. The capacity in 1995 was 800,000 tonnes. GEHL and the plant's management were not able to agree on a joint plan of action, which led to GEHL reducing its stake to 12.6% during 1995 from 28% in 1993 and in 1994, and settling for a guaranteed 15% return on investment. It was listed in April 1996, after selling 43.1mn A shares at Rmb3.60 per share to PRC investors. The company was also approved to issue B shares. Another steel plant invested in by the group is Shaoguan Steel, though its 5% stake makes it more of a passive investment.

In Shaoguan as well, GEHL holds a 60% stake (1994) in a cement plant with a design capacity of 800,000 tonnes in 1995. The cement plant, Changshan Cement Plant, began production in 1992 and a major capacity upgrade was completed in 1995. With the real estate market in the doldrums, production in 1995 was only 32% of the new design capacity.

Hotel operations

After transferring hotels in Hong Kong to the listed company's hotels and tours division in 1994, the group now operates hotels in Guangdong, Thailand and France. Management of these hotels falls under Jingmei Trading and Travel.

Infrastructure

Most infrastructure investments held by GEHL are concentrated in the Pearl River Delta and include bridges, highways and transport companies. An effective 20% stake in a joint investment with New World Infrastructure in a 129-km section of the Guangzhou-Zhuhai Expressway was sold to the listed company for HK$112mn in September 1996 (a related-party transaction). The project is expected to be completed in 1998.

Properties

Contributions from Guangdong and, to some extent Hong Kong, property development have been a drag on a number of companies since the region experienced a meltdown in the industry during 1994–95. GEHL has fared remarkably well in this environment, partly because its properties were bought in the 1980s, with little additional commitments made in the 1990s. In another related-party transaction in September 1996, the parent sold to its listed vehicle recently a 183,000 sq ft completed building in Western District on Hong Kong Island. The transaction was completed at an 8% discount to the appraised market value of HK$1.3bn.

Discussion of GDI operations

Without providing an exhaustive account of all subsidiaries, associates and investments, we focus here on a few of the major subsidiaries of GDI, including brewing and malting operations, the hotels and tours division, infrastructure, and the Tianhe shopping mall.

Industrial investments

Industrial operations, excepting a misadventure into the manufacture of washing machines, have proven to be among GDI's best investments. The most substantial include Shenzhen Brewery and Guangzhou Malt, which are undergoing expansion plans that will provide a for doubling of expansion by the end of 1996. Both the brewery, southern Guangdong's leading brewer, and malting operations will see their capacity reach 200,000 tonnes in 1997. An additional greenfield malting plant is being completed in Ningbo, which will produce 100,000 tonnes of malt beginning in 1997 and expand up to 200,000 tonnes in 1998. In 1997, about 13% of the bottom line will be generated by beer and malt. By 1998, this figure should reach 15%. Beer and malting operations were one of the more interesting assets of the group, and were listed on the Hong Kong Stock Exchange in July 1997. Other key industrials include a leather tannery in Hainan, Nanhai Tannery, a curtain wall installer, Full Arts, and a stake in a cement plant in Shaoguan.

Hotels and tours

Guangdong Investment has over 1,400 rooms under management in six hotels (including service apartments) in Hong Kong and one hotel in Shenzhen. The hotels contribute more to GDI's NAV than to its bottom line, as up to 70% of business is linked to the tours operation and its tours to Hong Kong for Chinese tourists on package tours. Rates per day for the rooms range between HK$400 and HK$1,000 (against over HK$2,200 for five-star hotel rooms in Hong Kong). The Wharney Hotel in Wanchai boasts the highest walk-in rate, with average rates in mid-1996 of about HK$870. In 1995, about 120,000 Chinese tourists came to Hong Kong using Guangdong Tours, representing a rather flat performance compared to 1994. China's austerity programme has not been kind to the tours business from Guangdong, despite the introduction of a five-day working week in mid-1995, which should have served to stimulate travel. As mentioned above, the division is also believed to engage in a substantial amount of trading in appliances.

Infrastructure

Two power plants, one toll road and one bridge fall under the division. Many of the projects represent investments in local government operations for a fixed return rather than a real commitment to developing and managing infrastructure projects. As such, rates of return should really be determined according to the credit standing of the organisations receiving the funds. The 300MW Shaoguan D plant acquired in 1994 has been one of the saving graces for the company. In 1995, the plant sold more electricity than its contracted 1.39bn kWh per year. The IRR has been brought as high as 20%, 5% more than the guaranteed rate. In early-and mid-1996, the company invested in a 12.5% stake in two Meixian 150MW power generators, one which began operation in late 1996 and one which was to be scheduled to be completed in mid-1997.

Property

This division has been somewhat of a black hole for the group, with plans for residential projects, such as Riverside Garden in Panyu (outside Guangzhou), facing constant changes. Nevertheless, the project's remaining phases have been successfully refocused on local buyers, with Guangdong Investment having decided that it was better to cut the profit margin in half than to wait for a new wave of Hong Kong buyers. The company wisely decided in 1994 to reduce its exposure to property. However, although the company may have wanted to classify the 1.7mn sq ft Tianhe shopping mall under the category of retail, GDI's major property play has been an estimated HK$1.5bn investment in this project. Tianhe City began operations in February 1996, with Nanfang Department Store being the first major retailer to open its doors there.

Retail

In mid-1995 GDI acquired a 56% stake in Nanfang Department Store, Guangdong's leading retailer. This subsidiary will provide strong contributions at some stage after mid-1997. However, to the surprise of quite a few observers, the department store turned in a loss on operations during most of 1996. The Tianhe mall in northeast Guangzhou is managed under Guangdong Teem, which has been acting as a coordinator for many of the companies coming into the complex. The mall is directed at upscale shoppers, and is expected to become a Mecca for shoppers in Guangzhou, particularly toward the year 2000. Over the short term, despite a good start for Tianhe Mall in Spring 1996, a number of obstacles will cloud operations over the early years of the mall, not the least of which will be an over-supply of property in the Tianhe district.

Conclusion: what next for the group?

The principal challenge ahead for the listed company is to develop hands-on managerial skills over its existing subsidiaries. Growth in Guangdong will outperform that of China less and less. The cost of capital and taxes is on the rise, and there are no more ready-made cash cows to acquire from the parent. Immediate attention must be given to reversing weak cash flow, both at the parent and at the listed company.

Guangdong Investment, to be fair, does have some redeeming qualities. Its management puts significant effort into investor relations. The company listens to its investors and tries to aim its development plans based on what they want. To this end, Guangdong Investment took on a new managing director in early 1997. One of the first items on the agenda appeared to be improving share price performance compared to other leading red chips. By May 1997, the listed company had sent the message to investors that it was back in action with a spin-off for its Shenzhen brewery division. At the same time, a cursory look at a release of the 1996 annual report in May 1997 underscored that the group's stretched cash flow position remained as weak as in previous reports. The challenges for the group making it into the 21st century will be dictated by how seriously management deals with cash flow and its significant number of problem businesses. In looking at the relationship between the holding and listed companies, one can not help but think that Guangdong Investment and Guangdong Enterprises share some similarities with Oscar Wilde's *The Picture of Dorian Gray* — and that some day the picture in the attic will come back to haunt its rightful owner.

CHAPTER 8

Challenges to reforming China's steel industry

David Sakmar

Reform of the state sector has not been uniform from industry to industry. The steel industry remains one of China's most highly state-controlled and least profitable sectors. The experiences of the steel industry as it grapples with reforming inefficient behemoth state enterprises provides a useful example of the more general problem of shifting from a socialist to a more market-based economy.

Most steel companies are not red chips. Notable exceptions are the Shougang group of companies, which entered the Hong Kong stock exchange via back-door listings. Other red chip steel-related companies also include CNNC (China National Non-Ferrous Metals Industry Corp) companies such as Oriental Metals, which is principally a copper and other non-ferrous metals trading company. Simsen Metals, listed in 1994 as a window company for the local Shenzhen arm of CNNC, is a non-ferrous metals trading and mining company as well. For the real steel companies, which represent the epitome of China's state-owned enterprises, investors must turn listed H shares such as Maanshan Steel and Angang Steel.

This chapter analyses the Chinese steel industry as it operates within the Ministry of Metallurgical Industry, concentrating on the workings of Chinese State Owned Enterprises (SOEs) operating within the special steel sector of the Chinese economy, and comes from the experiences of working executives dealing and doing business with these Chinese companies. The intent is to provide some historical perspective on the development and workings of an industry functioning within a socialist or state-planned economy, together with a practical, hands-on case study of the behaviour of Chinese SOEs operating in a particular industry.

China's steel industry: historical development and origins

China's steel sector and the heavy industrial sector in general, owe much of their development and origin to the Stalinist model of corporate formation and structure. After the establishment of the PRC in 1949, the Chinese Communist Party set about immediately with a programme to rebuild and strengthen the country. China had been devastated by the Second World War and its own civil war between the Nationalists and Communists. Much of its industry, already primitive, lay in ruins. The late 1940s and early 1950s were a period of great tension between China and the Western capitalist world, and the Communists initially sought to rebuild and modernise the country's defence and industrial base, including power generation, transportation and machinery. In this the central government saw the metallurgical industry as the pillar of the national economy.

Practically speaking, steel production was crucial to the rebuilding of the country's industrial infrastructure. And from an ideological standpoint, the Communists used the production of steel as a yardstick by which to measure its competition with the West. The Communists equated the number of tonnes/year of steel production as a symbol of China's national development. There was a slogan from the central government in the 1950s that captured this sentiment: *"Chao Yingguo gan Meiguo"*, which meant "Surpass Great Britain, catch the United States". The party set as a goal matching Western steel production within a ten-year period, and directed a large amount of national investment toward the metallurgical industry beginning in the 1950s.

During this period, the quality of Chinese steel was very low. Equipment and metallurgical practices were primitive, limiting the steel industry to the production of low-carbon steels, pig iron, and other basic products. China could not produce advanced, high alloyed steels necessary for the production of components in defence and aerospace applications. Throughout the 1950s, 1960s and 1970s, therefore, China embarked on massive imports of steel-making facilities and equipment.

Also during this period, Mao's Third Front policy of National Defence had substantial effects upon the Chinese special steel industry. To create a "third front" against Western attack, China located or relocated critical defence and industrial infrastructure to remote areas of China's interior. From an economic standpoint, this programme was a disaster hindering China's metallurgical industry to this day. For example, Changcheng Special Steel Plant and Zhongyuan Special Steel, part of the a larger industrial infrastructure outside Sichuan and Henan Provinces, are basically isolated in very mountainous regions, where communication, transportation and logistics are virtually impossible. This also makes reforming these SOEs all the more difficult, because any reduction in employment due to restructuring cannot be supported by other industries in the region and would create massive social upheaval.

In the 1980s China made great strides in upgrading the metallurgical industry's technical and manufacturing conditions. The state government contributed a second wave of investment into the metallurgical industry. For example, Baoshan Steel imported advanced Japanese steel-making equipment and practices. Wuhan Iron and Steel, Taiyuan Iron and Steel, and Fushun Steel Plant all installed state of the art equipment and facilities imported from Japan, Germany, Austria and the United States. Specific equipment imported included advanced ladle refining furnaces, high speed forging presses, and high temperature heat treatment facilities capable of producing materials to stricter standards.

Through these investments, the Chinese steel industry not only increased the quantity of production, but altered the product mix from low-end steels (low carbon) to higher-end products (high- and super-alloy products). This meant that in addition to basic infrastructure requirements, China could now produce critical-application parts for aerospace, energy and power generation. Although the United States and China were still adversaries in the Cold War, many of these components had been imported from Eastern Europe, Austria, Sweden and Japan. Ironically, China got much of what it needed from the United States' allies.

This was significant in that it represented a move away from the Soviet model of state planning and metallurgical industry. This model was rejected in the mid-1960s, in part due to larger political struggles between China and the Soviet Union, and for more technical reasons particular to the metallurgical industry. Chinese steel experts also realised the limitations of the Soviet model. The West had already leaped ahead of the Soviet Union in steel-making technology. China realised these developments and began to adjust its own metallurgical industry in this direction.

Characteristics of the Stalinist model in the steel industry

In the Stalinist model, the state government set specific objectives (such as number of tonnes/year) in annual meetings between the State Planning Commission and metallurgical industry executives. The conclusions of these meetings became the final production plan that would be distributed to individual mills. Investment in plant and equipment would be matched with these production targets.

An obvious weakness of this system was that production hardly correlated to market conditions and demands. A less obvious weakness was that the plan was fixed for a one year period. Once the plan was drawn up, it could not be changed until the next year's meeting, with a semi-annual adjustment. The mills, therefore, lacked the flexibility to adjust, even when it was clear to executives that they should. A further weakness was that all production prices were fixed for the year by the State Planning Commission. Prices of raw materials, energy, and finished products were set in the plan, and could not be changed.

Until the end of the 1970s, all annual plans were completely fixed and dominated the entire production of steel mills in China. One hundred percent of China's steel production was determined by an annual state plan. The mills had no flexibility to adjust to market conditions of over or under supply. Beginning in the late 1970s, the state government began to turn to a more market-focused system. The enterprises in the metallurgical industry were given more flexibility with 5% of production sold on the open market. This ratio was adjusted upwards over the years, to the point that today each mill has control over all of its production.

Relationship with the Ministry of Metallurgical Industry

Since the 1950s, the steel industry has operated under the auspices of the Ministry of Metallurgical Industry. The relationship between the ministry and individual steel mills has changed over the years, with the ministry having less and less of a say in how each firm operates. In the 1950s and 1960s, ministry bureaucrats controlled each mill's finances, personnel and production management completely. The ministry had absolute power and was responsible for training, selecting and appointing individuals to top managerial positions in the mills. The ministry determined an individual firm's business policies, monitored performance, and determined and targeted investment in equipment and market development. This began to change during the 1970s, such that today, the ministry really only has the suggestive power to advise and counsel. It exercises a weaker version of Japanese ministries' "administrative guidance", familiar to observers of Asian capitalism.

However, the ministry still has the right to make suggestions regarding appointments of the top leadership in the mills, consulting with provincial or municipal governments in some cases, and with central government officials in other instances, depending upon the specific enterprise. These leaders typically are chosen from within the metallurgical industry, with the top leadership of China's steel enterprises rotated among enterprises. The majority of these leaders were trained and educated in one of the several prominent technical and/or metallurgical institutes in China.

The actual amount of power any individual mill president has can vary, however, depending upon that individual's reputation, ability and influence with local and provincial governments. Manufacturing operations that can generate greater tax revenue and employment at the local level will enjoy greater flexibility both from the ministry and provincial leadership. In practice, enterprises submit business and financial reports on a regular basis to the ministry.

In the past, the ministry acted as each steel enterprise's primary source of investment capital in return for political allegiance. Today, however, most enterprises exercise a greater degree of control over their working capital and administrative funds. Nevertheless, during the 1993–95 austerity measures instituted by Beijing, working-capital allocations underwent a period of recentralisation, leaving state-administered commercial banks with insufficient funds to inject into most SOEs. This meant that even if particular enterprises had enough capital to pursue expansion projects, a wide cross-section of their clients had insufficient funds on hand to pay their obligations. This phenomenon, known as triangular debt, left many enterprises no choice but to reduce the amount of business coming from clients with non-performing receivables. Looking beyond the effects of the most recent austerity drive by Beijing, however, only large-scale metallurgical projects, which are proposed, approved and funded at the State Council and ministerial level, remain under direct control of the ministry.

The decision-making calculus for determining the type and extent of investment appears to place more stress on the capabilities the central government believes are important to acquire, rather than market research to identify what the market may be demanding. Factory management implements and manages investments in plant and equipment, but the actual determination of the type and capability is still made in Beijing.

Anatomy of a state-owned enterprise in the steel sector

The central government is constantly rotating provincial leaders of top enterprises, to avoid having any individual build up a power base in his area. However, top leaders of enterprises can retain power if they achieve profitability, or continue contributing to local government officials. Experts in certain industries can remain in power past retirement age and to recommend certain appointments.

Deputy positions in the enterprise are recommended by a research group within a committee made up of enterprise personnel, the chairman usually being the enterprise's president or managing director. The committee recommends the appointment of top deputy managers to the municipal government. The subdivision managers are recommended to the top leader by the personnel department of the mill.

The Communist Party keeps political control while allowing the mill operating autonomy. Each enterprise has a party secretary nominated by municipal and provincial government officials. The nominee is then "elected" by the workers in the factory. This preserves and assures the Party of control, while maintaining the appearance of unanimity in decision making. Though the party secretary typically holds a working title, he or she usually does not have metallurgical or technical training and is generally not involved in the day to day administration of the factory.

In the past, subdivision managers and working personnel were selected for their political allegiance and loyalty. As a result of the reform policies of the early 1980s, SOEs have gradually been encouraged to operate as profit-maximising entities. In theory, the incentive structure should reward managerial ability and efficiency. However, in practice, although more stress is placed on issues of profitability, political loyalty is still the deciding factor in selecting managers.

Although top managers in China's SOEs are not well paid, they do have certain rewards and perks that make these positions desirable, such as free housing, security and maid services. They have access to the company's automobiles and can travel freely, and can provide their relatives with better economic and employment opportunities. There is also the rather ubiquitous under-the-table compensation, which can be substantial. These rewards insure that competition from within the industry for senior management positions is keen. They do not guarantee, however, that top management within the large SOEs is capable. Accountability among senior managers in China is still very weak. They do not face the scrutiny of efficient capital markets that forces managers of OECD multinationals to produce profits.

Ultimately, top leaders of industry maintain their position by contributing tax revenue to the local and/or provincial government. Therefore, they must balance political loyalty among subordinates with capability. In practice, most senior management are more interested in their personal financial benefit. The link between enterprise performance and top management performance is not always clear. Certainly, successful enterprises, for whatever reason, will allow senior management more flexibility in utilising enterprise funds.

It is difficult to generalise about the "typical" SOE in the steel industry. Although each company is theoretically subject to similar constraints and regulations, companies do end up behaving with different "personalities" depending upon the location of the factory, the background and reputation of the top leadership, and other factors. A factory that has a capable and strong top leader can be very effective in minimizing bureaucracy and achieving a high degree of manufacturing efficiency. It may not be acting as a true profit maximiser, but it certainly can produce high quality products with reliable deliveries and good service. The factory that has weak leadership, on the other hand, can rarely meet manufacturing standards even remotely approaching Western efficiency. The bureaucracy is so entrenched, and the management so risk averse, that price and profit really are irrelevant. Higher prices will not promote better performance for these firms.

The interplay between politics and enterprise management at the local level is also crucial. Although they are appointed by the central government, top enterprise leaders have strong incentives to work closely with local political officials, who invariably try to protect their resources and people. For example, taxes are supposed to be paid to the central government, accumulated from the province's state enterprises. However, government officials help state enterprises to hide profits, in return for direct payments to local government officials. Thus, though the central government may actually want to reform state enterprises, they are often undermined at the provincial level. Most SOEs do not want to do Beijing's dirty work and risk incurring the wrath of provincial officials. Top enterprise leaders ultimately are held accountable by the local people and government, even if on paper they are appointed by the ministry.

These factors are clearly significant to the business executive attempting to sort good from bad among SOEs in the steel sector, and do business in China. In our experience, we located several steel mills, all of which exhibited the technical and manufacturing capabilities of producing our products. However, after much effort and costly trial and error, it became apparent that only those firms with strong, even dictatorial, top leaders, had the personal authority and drive to force their enterprise personnel to meet international standards.

In state-owned enterprises, the government is obviously the majority shareholder. Depending upon the enterprise, the central or provincial government, or a combination of both, may hold primary control. With the larger, integrated steel mills, including Shougang, Anshan Steel, Wuhan Steel, and Baoshan, the central government exercises control over these national enterprises. The smaller, regional mills operate under more provincial control, and generally are more flexible and less bureaucratic. With the liberalisation of the economy, many semi-private and/or partially reformed state enterprises have implemented a rigid system of rewards. These conditions differ widely among particular enterprises in China's steel sector, however. South China appears to have a greater concentration of enterprises operating profitably, with several private enterprises highly efficient, even by international standards.

Although SOEs still are predominant in China's steel industry, there is a growing private sector. It is difficult to gather data regarding these enterprises because by their nature they are quite independent of central government and ministerial supervision. In the special steel industry there are at least four private enterprises in China operating with ISO 9000 certificates. These private companies have an ownership structure similar to Western employee-owned corporations. Typically, though in theory these enterprises are owned by employees, the owner has strong control. These enterprises tend to be smaller, less integrated operations. Equipment and facilities are generally not as advanced as SOEs, however, they appear to run more efficiently and are better managed. They definitely operate as profit maximisers, though from our experience, most of these profits end up in the pocket of the owner. Of the factories visited, one mill owner had an elaborate house almost as large as his factory.

Prospects for reform and the future of SOEs

Since the mid 1970s, China has been on a long road toward restructuring its economy away from a centrally planned, state-owned system, toward a more market-based economy. Beginning with agriculture, China's top leaders have adopted a deliberate, if lengthy, reform process aimed at gradually reducing the impact of the state sector on the overall economy. It has been a delicate balancing act, weighing the desire for increased efficiency against the necessity of preserving social stability.

Reform of the state sector, in general, has proceeded slowly, with the proportion of SOEs versus private companies as a whole decreasing in China in recent years. However, reform has not taken place uniformly among industries, and the influence of the state sector is still pervasive. SOEs still account for over 40% of industrial production, and by some estimates, distort the allocation of as much as 70% of China's resources. Although some have become internationally competitive, particularly light industry in southern China, the proportion of SOEs operating in the steel and heavy industry sectors remains high. Up through 1996, the central government has been slow to implement privatisation, and in instances where it has, the results have not been encouraging (Shougang, Maanshan Steel). These mills, and others, have been reluctant or unable to implement and institutionalise true reforms, making steel one of the least profitable industries in China.

There are several reasons for this. First, the steel industry, in state-controlled, command-type economies like China and the former Soviet Union, has long been viewed as a priority industry, characterised by state ownership of assets, large bureaucracies, heavy subsidies, and limited or no attempts at profit maximizing. For political and military reasons, Stalin in the 1930s concentrated vast resources on developing a world-class heavy industry. China, too, during the 1950s and 1960s established national campaigns targeting the buildup of a heavy industrial infrastructure, with steel production a central part. The Great Leap Forward, and more recently, the Third Front Defence Industrialisation Programme of the 1960s and 1970s built up state-owned industrial infrastructure in northeastern and southern China. Steel mills were, and continue to be, an integral part of these developments, and from a practical standpoint it is probably impossible to attempt reform of a single sector or industry without undertaking reform of the entire industrial framework.

Second, an entire bureaucratic infrastructure was developed, and a generation of leaders trained, under the Stalinist model. Today, the majority of top steel executives, those running the larger, integrated mills, are in their late fifties or early sixties, studied metallurgy in university in the 1950s, lived or trained under Russian tutelage, speak Russian rather than English, and basically continue to run their factories under the only economic and management model for which they were trained. They do receive continued training under the auspices of the Ministry of Metallurgy, but again, most ministry officials received their training in the former Soviet Union.

Very few top executives, during their formative university and post-graduate training, received exposure to Western metallurgical and engineering ideas. Clearly, the Ministry of Metallurgy has worked in recent years to introduce more free-market thinking in its push to convert SOEs into more private, profit-conscious enterprises. Most top leaders have attended seminars in privatisation, capital markets, "Western" management, and so on. In theory, this means that they should have the conceptual flexibility to create more flexible, efficient organisations. In reality, there is still a great deal of intellectual and personal baggage preventing sustainable improvements in most SOEs in the steel sector.

Compounding the problem is a generational lack of leadership. The Cultural Revolution so decimated the ranks of China's trained populace that most large steel companies, in our experience, lack a level of management that would have been trained in non-Soviet methods during the 1960s were it not for the Cultural Revolution. The result is that in most enterprises, the top leadership is aging, with only few mid-forties executives to assume leadership. This problem has made the older generation more reluctant to change or leave, and left the younger generation with the talent and training to implement reform, but not the power. They are still in very junior-level positions with little decision-making authority.

Third, because the steel industry is so capital intensive, and under traditional steel-making processes, is characterised by economies of scale in production, a large amount of state control has been necessary in supporting these industries during their formation. This was true in the United States, Japan and Germany, and both Stalin and Mao realised that in order to catch up to the West, substantial resources had to be diverted from agriculture to heavy industry. It has only been in recent years, even in the more advanced steel-making countries like the United States, Japan and Germany, that production techniques have moved away from large integrated mills toward more decentralised manufacturing operations.

The US steel industry went through an extremely severe and painful restructuring in the 1980s, the Japanese in the late 1980s and early 1990s, and Germany in the 1990s. These examples suggest that the steel industry is difficult to reform even in capitalist economies. The Chinese steel industry, as was the Soviet Union's, has been burdened by a combination of excessive reliance on planned models of development and almost no personal or corporate accountability, and a highly conservative mindset. In short, a reformer's nightmare.

Lastly, on a more practical level, the manufacturing environment of most steel mills is highly inflexible. From a facilities and equipment standpoint, much of what Chinese steel mills utilise was designed to meet Soviet metallurgical concepts and standards. For example, ingot mould patterns used by all steel mills in the Chinese special steel industry were patterned after Russian octagonal types that for a variety of reasons are poorly designed for melting high-alloy steels. The design offers poor metallurgical properties, results in lower quality product, and is less efficient to work with. Support equipment, then, was constructed around these ingot types, making the entire factory, therefore, hostage to a poor initial production concept. To improve the efficiency of the mill would require a redesigned ingot mould, and also a large-scale overhaul of manufacturing support equipment. Vested interests of various sorts act to prevent this type of change from occurring. Most mills have very large technical and research and development departments, employing up to several thousand people. Many of these research departments would not admit that their ingot mould is the cause of many metallurgical problems.

Incentive structures within state enterprises contribute greatly to the "software" challenges of reform that are, perhaps, more intractable than those "hardware" issues mentioned above. The political nature of personnel decision-making within state enterprises limits the rewards for risk taking and responsibility. It, therefore, promotes extreme caution among managers, a stifling bureaucracy, and low efficiency. The reward for a risky project successfully completed may be a pat on the back and limited financial benefit. However, the cost of failure is likely to be castigation, removal, or even imprisonment in certain cases. The committee structure common within state enterprises, practically means that everyone has the right to veto a business idea or proposal, but no one is protected or encouraged to promote risky, but potentially profitable, business ventures.

Contradictory laws and regulations, both within state enterprises and within the Chinese economy in general, also contribute to inherent conservatism among enterprises. Though it is well known that Westerners often find the Chinese legal system obscure, the Chinese, themselves, are increasingly confused by the plethora of new laws handed down by the central government. Many of these laws, especially concerning the protection of individual rights, are not regularly monitored and are poorly enforced. Managers eventually realise that though the central government supposedly encourages entrepreneurial behaviour and risk taking, failure within an enterprise often means the end of one's career. This type of system ultimately promotes cynicism, corruption and irrational decision-making, all-pervasive among China's state enterprises. It is in a larger sense a type of "religious crisis", or what Fukuyama has labelled "social trust", that cannot easily be remedied by traditional economic reform.

Appendices

Appendix 8A: Steel production

8.1: Steel production in the Deng era (1975–95)

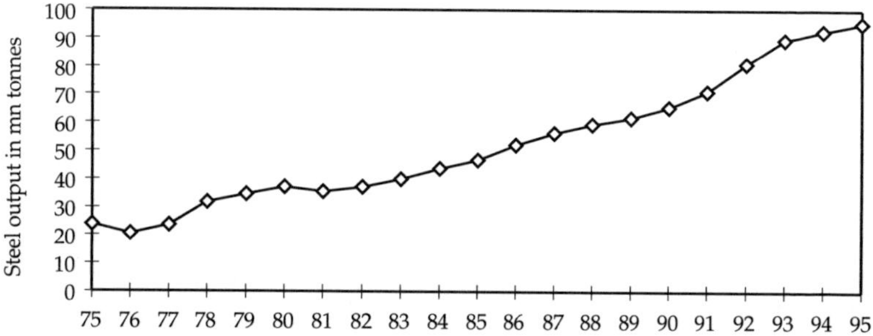

Source: China Steel Yearbook 1994; CSY 1996

8.2: Increase in GDP and steel production 1985–95

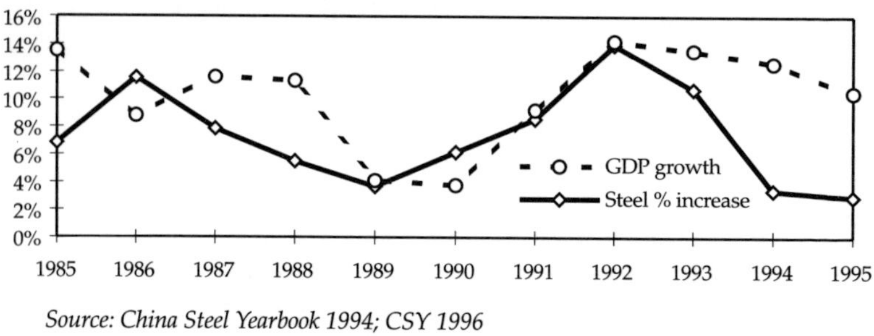

Source: China Steel Yearbook 1994; CSY 1996

Appendix 8B: Steel manufacturers

Table 8.1
Largest Chinese steel-makers and comparative statistics

Rank	Enterprise	Steel prodn	Est. staff
1	Anshan Iron & Steel	8.51 mn tonnes	12,169
2	Shougang Steel	7.02	63,364
3	Baoshan Steel	6.98	na
4	Wuhan Steel	5.24	25,373
5	Baotou Steel	3.08	na
6	Benxi Steel	2.57	10,509
7	Panzhihua Steel	2.42	26,090
8	Shanghai No.1 Steel	2.41	na
9	Maanshan Steel	2.13	39,210
10	Taiyuan Steel	2.12	39,130

Source: Yearbook of Iron and Steel Industry of China (1994)

Epilogue

Charles de Trenck

Of the companies surveyed in this book, very few will mature into world-class companies either soon or with ease. The Chinese government's latest plan is to create large "model corporates" to provide role models for other Chinese companies.

This development is not as new as some may think. It does not fit neatly into an explanation claiming that China is moving toward emulating large Korean and Japanese conglomerates (which are proving not to be ideal models in light of recent bankruptcy scares). Neither does it point to invocation of pure administrative models along the lines of Japan's MITI. The restructuring of China's large state-held companies, even of holding companies at the State Council level (which in turn control the red chips in Hong Kong), also has roots in China's socialist past.

Many state companies are currently undergoing continued corporatisation exercises, aimed, prima facie, at further reducing links with the state. But at the same time as direct relations with the state are severed, there appears to be a concurrent move to centralise. The process of centralising in China in the late 1990s could mean the following: 1) a move to create larger more competitive companies; or 2) an attempt to introduce more regimentation of a number of "variables" that have at times run loose during the early- and mid-1990s, ranging from senior executives to pricing policies; or 3) a move to develop China's own answer to MITI.

Most likely is that China has created a hybrid. This hybrid model of centralising and creating larger companies is taking on unlikely bedfellows and appears to further reinforce the argument set out in the introduction to this book — which is that there is little capitalism, as it is understood in OECD countries, at work in China at present.

Having said this, there are some enterprises distinguishing themselves in this painful process. But they are few and far between and not necessarily characterised by size or name recognition. Top picks for China's best-managed companies include:

CITIC Pacific, China Resources, and COSCO. Of these CITIC Pacific is arguably not a pure Chinese company at all, as has been well documented in this and other publications. Most other companies, though perceived externally as being of the same calibre as the three named above, are still not in the same class when it comes to organisational structure.

SEPTEMBER 1997

Epilogue, part II

Following the last revision of this book in early Fall '97, the onset of the "Asian crisis" has taken its toll on most Asian regional markets and economies. Readers and investors have speculated and wondered about China's susceptibility to being buffeted by the same forces that brought down the "Asian tigers". Of greatest concern has been to what extent would China trade growth slow down and when would there be a devaluation of the Rmb to allow China to compete with other Asian countries that have seen demand for their manufactured goods increase (in volume if not in US dollar terms).

The fact is that there are many concerns to be entertained with respect to China's economy and companies. But following an impulsive logic that China must suffer the same problems as other Asian countries is not likely to solve the problems at hand — which continue to be the same issues as those raised in this book and, of course, the ongoing problem of SOE reform.

Since our first edition came out, and following the outcome of the March 1998 Ninth Peoples' Congress, Zhu Rongji was elected Premier and ministerial and SOE reform plans have been revised further. Additional red chips have also been listed on the Hong Kong stock exchange, with the most prominent listing being China Telecom in late October 1997.

Zhu Rongji initiated a number of reforms of companies and government ministries, all of which are aimed at reducing red tape and staff levels. With respect to red chips, one burning issue that in March and April 1998 was still unresolved was the impact that ministerial reform would have on listed red chips. Initial views from analysts ranged from "positive for some" to "negative for most". My own view is that although the issue is important and some listed companies will be impacted in terms of perception, and perhaps even in real terms, the bigger issue relating to management quality transcends the issue of who the immediate parent is.

In other words, the announcement by the government that 11 of 40 ministries would be dissolved and/or merged into others is expected to lead to some changes for listed red chips. Examples of companies undergoing such change have so far come from listed H shares such as Yizheng Chemical Fibre and China Shipping Development. Both of these merger stories were conceptually appealing when they appeared in mid-1997. But both mergers had, as of early April 1998, failed to deliver anything but complex corporate transactions offering little added value to shareholders. The problem was not in the intention, but in the execution and in the valuations.

Going forward, the issue for red chips may very well be one of just which red chips are we talking about. Red chips considered in better positions to capitalise on government restructuring, as well as belonging to a "new breed" of red chip, include companies such as China Telecom, Legend and CNPC.

New and rising red chip companies will in future more likely be associated with either a region or an industry rather than with a ministry. This trend represents an important outcome of ongoing reforms, with notable exceptions including companies such as China Resources (under MOFTEC), which are likely to remain leading conglomerates. One apparent very recent outcome of on-going reforms will be changes in reporting lines (shifts from ministry to ministry, or to another entity). But at the end of the exercise, management quality will determine how well red chips fare in restructured China.

APRIL 1998

Red chips: A call for action

Charles de Trenck

What developed countries generally call "capitalism" still does not exist among large companies in China. In its place, there has been financial engineering dominated by intra-group transactions. I propose to categorise the phenomenon under the term "cut-and-paste capitalism". The most well-known form is that practiced by red chips in Hong Kong and centring on acquisitions of assets held by China and Hong Kong parents through share issues and bank loans.

Red chip growth through asset acquisition and injections has been the most visible example of Chinese cut-and-paste capitalism at work. Most of the transactions realised over the last several years have been through related party transactions (intra-group transactions between unlisted arms and listed arms). As such, the majority of acquisitions have been part of an equitisation of unlisted parents' assets, which are typically very highly geared, through Hong Kong–listed red chip vehicles. On balance, these intra-group transactions have had a positive impact on share price performance of the listed vehicles — and investors have therefore benefited up to now. In 1996, red chip index outperformance of the Hang Seng Index was 96%, and in 1997 it was 13%. (In August 1997 outperformance was as high as 110% before falling back by year end.)

But what has been the basis for superior share price performance has not been enhancement of shareholder value so much as 1) the expansion of market capitalisation through new share issues, which has allowed institutional investors to participate in these vehicles as a proxy for investing in China; 2) the presentation of a good and easy to understand story, which has provided for an added boost to the issue of new shares; and 3) a willing public.

Red chips have not yet proven they understand the responsibilities of being cutting-edge Chinese corporations. On a valuations basis they have created more intangibles based on the accounting concept of goodwill than they have enhanced their shareholders' interests through successful business strategies in the sense of value creation.

As a result of following a cut-and-paste approach to building their listed vehicles, red chips have been deal-flow driven and typically have shunned organic growth and strategic acquisitions based on industry specialisation. Both transactions and valuations have tended toward packages designed to look good on an earnings basis, but not on a cash-flow basis.

The standard practice for many injections has been to inject greater than 20% and less than 51% stakes in key assets. This percentage of total earnings of the acquired assets is booked, despite the fact that dividends paid, the actual cash flow, are usually far lower than the equity-accounted earnings. In other words, there often is little control over the asset and there is little cash flow either. Of course, there are exceptions to this practice. But the acquisition of non-contolling and low real cash flow assets is an issue that investors must focus on seriously.

The worst perpetrators have been companies that issued new equity for non-focussed acquisitions which later turned sour. Guangdong Investment's mid-1990s acquisitions of Guangdong property at the peak of the market and Hong Kong hotel assets that have generated mediocre performances provide an illustration of a high profile company that has placed new shares for assets that disappointed in following years. Since its misadventures top management sought to reinvigorate itself with new and younger hires. But as an example of using cut-and-paste capitalism in a more positive aspect, China Resources injected low-cost property assets and enhanced them after injection — to the benefit of minority shareholders.

Either way, over the longer term, red chips have to move away from cut-and-paste red chip capitalism simply because good parent assets to inject will dry up. Investor appetite for injections in late 1997 and early 1998, of course, remains shell-shocked from the steep Asian market sell-offs of 2H97. Red chips which survive the onslaught of the Hong Kong property slowdown, the restructuring of the Chinese economy and the general rise in the cost of capital following the Asian crisis will be those taking immediate action to streamline their corporate structures.

For red chip companies to succeed over the longer term, there must be one management team at the top looking down on one corporate structure — not multiple assemblies of independent subsidiaries pledging a loose allegiance to the group name and claiming some of the group's assets. Multiple senior-management structures have led to countless examples of duplication and even of open rivalry. For China's leading companies to take the next bold step forward towards becoming multinationals, each group must put forth one principal management team to be held accountable to minority shareholders. Furthermore, regional offices must be linked through computing facilities, unified strategic and global policy formulation must be instituted and financial incentives and career path opportunities for capable staff should be offered. The time to act is now.

Further data

Here we present information not specific to single chapters.

Table X.1: China's top 20 foreign-funded enterprises

(sales & profits in Rmb mn)

		Sales	Pre-tax profit
1	Shanghai Volkswagen	12,710.4	1,006.7
2	Shanghai Bell Telephone	5,155.0	1,160.7
3	Nanhai Oil & Fats (Chiwan)	4,320.0	238.0
4	Beijing Jeep	4,127.4	255.8
5	Chongqing Qingling Auto	2,704.5	501.8
6	Motorola (China)	2,570.6	n.a.
7	Shenzhen Konka Electronics	2,386.8	368.7
8	Shenzhen Lianxing Computer	2,361.7	13.0
9	Beijing Matsushita TV Picture Tube	2,328.9	413.1
10	Shanghai Fenhuang Bicycles	2,310.0	131.6
11	Shanghai Vacuum	2,261.2	91.1
12	Shanghai Mitsubishi	2,202.9	261.4
13	Shanghai Dajiang	2,035.2	180.9
14	Guangzou P&G	1,941.9	845.4
15	Huaqiang Sanyo Electronics	1,916.9	35.0
16	Fujian Yong-en Group	1,910.0	74.5
17	Guangzhou Steel	1,892.6	98.9
18	Guangdong Rongsheng Refrigerator	1,838.7	230.0
19	Shanghai Ek-Chor Motorcycle	1,828.8	198.9
20	Guangxi Yuchai Machinery	1,802.2	510.9

Source: China Economic Monthly, 1994

X.1: US$-Rmb exchange rates

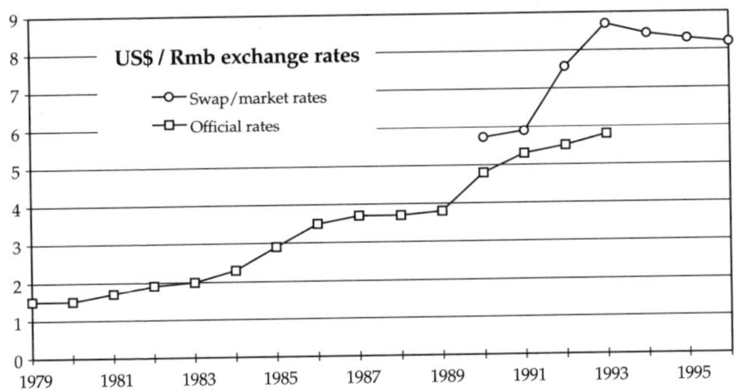

Source: PBOC

Table X.2: China 's largest industrials & trading companies

	Industrials	Trading companies
1	Daqing Petroleum	Sinochem
2	Yuxi Cigarette Factory	CEROIL Food
3	East China Power Corp	China National Tech I/E Corp
4	Baoshan Steel	China National Metals I/E Corp
5	Shougang Steel	China National Textiles I/E Corp
6	Shanghai Automobile	China National Air Material Corp
7	Anshan Iron	China National Electronics I/E Corp
8	China No. 1 Auto	Chian National Mach I/E Corp
9	North China Power	China North Industries
10	China Huazhong Power	China Petrochem International Facilities

Source: China Economic Monthly, 1994

Table X.3: Selected China funds

Fund	Issue size *(US$mn)*	Issue date
BOC China Fund	154.00	1/11/92
Cathay Invst Fund	9.31	1/10/92
China Assets (Holdings)	9.57	1/4/92
China Invst. Co.	26.70	1/5/92
China Invst Trust	16	1/5/93
China Invst & Dvlpt Fund	82.0	1/10/92
China & Eastern Invst Trust	17.0	1/11/95
China Fund Inc	148.9	1/5/92
China Fund Ltd	46.0	1/4/92
Chine Invst. 2000	10.0	1/8/92
Fleming Chinese Invst Trust	60	1/10/93
Greater China Fund Inc	214.1	1/7/92
HSBC China Fund Ltd	11.7	1/6/92
Invst Co China	66.2	na
JF China Invst Co.	26.0	1/8/87
JF China Region Fund Ltd	124.5	1/10/93
KWR China Fund	60.0	1/10/92
Lloyd George SC China	45.4	1/7/92
SHK Pearl River Delta Invst Co	9.7	1991
Shanghai Fund (Caymen)	19.4	1/7/92
Shanghai Growth	96.0	1/11/93
Templeton China World Fund	211.5	1/9/93
Templeton Dragon	810.0	1/9/94

Sources: fund prospectuses

China's imports and exports by region

X.2: China's exports by region, 1995

1995 Exports - US$148.8bn

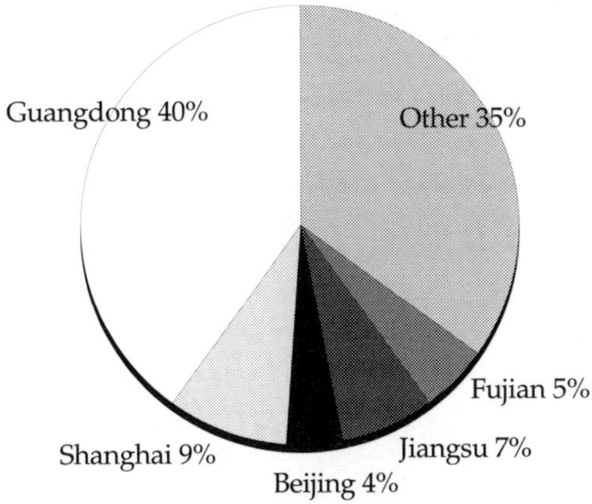

Source: China Statistical Yearbook, 1996

X.3: China's imports by region, 1995

1995 Imports - US$132.0bn

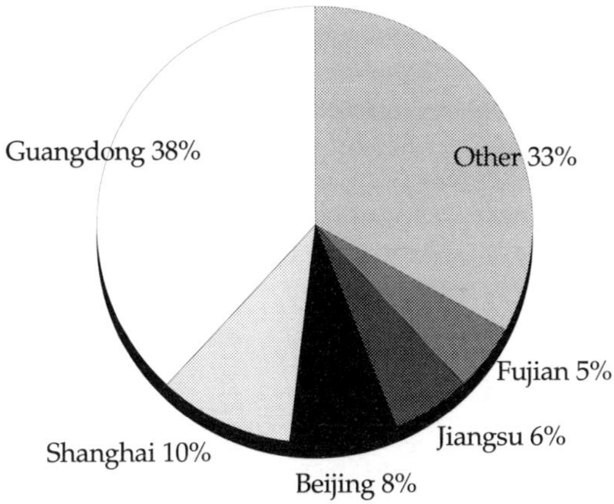

Source: China Statistical Yearbook, 1996

Table X.4: Hong Kong–listed H Shares as at May 1997

Company	**Sector**	**Date listed**	**Funds raised** *(US$mn)*	**Listing P/E** *(Fully diluted)*	**IPO price** *(HK$)*
Shanghai Petrochem	Petrochemicals	1/7/93	343	14.4	1.58
Tsingtao Brewery	Beverages	1/7/93	125	17.9	2.80
Beiren Printing	Machinery	1/8/93	26	11.5	2.08
Guangzhou Ship	Maritime constr.	1/8/93	42	9.8	2.08
Kunming Machine	Machinery	1/12/93	16	10.6	1.98
Maanshan Steel	Building materials	1/11/93	508	9.8	2.27
Yizheng Chemical[1]	Petrochemicals	1/3/94	308	13.8	2.38
Tianjin Bohai	Petrochemicals	1/5/94	53	12.6	1.20
Dongfang Electrical	Power/machinery	1/5/94	62	11.9	2.83
Luoyang Glass	Building materials	1/7/94	118	10.5	3.65
Qingling Auto	Automotive	1/8/94	134	9.0	2.31
Haixing Shipping	Shipping	1/11/94	204	10.8	1.46
Zhenhai Refining	Petrochemicals	1/12/94	185	14.4	2.38
Chengdu Telecom	Telecom equip.	1/12/94	58	13.1	2.80
Harbin Power	Power/machinery	1/12/94	145	14.7	2.58
Jilin Chemical	Petrochemicals	1/5/95	194	8.4	1.76
Northeast Electrical	Power/equipment	1/6/95	57	9.1	1.80
Jingwei Textile Machinery	Textile/machinery	1/1/96	27	7.3	1.29
Nanjing Panda	Electronics/TVs	1/4/96	67	7.5	2.13

Table X.4: Hong Kong–listed H Shares as at May 1997

Company	Sector	Date listed	Funds raised (US$mn)	Listing P/E (Fully diluted)	IPO price (HK$)
Guangshen Railway	Transport/railway	1/5/96	542	11.7	2.93
Guangdong Kelon	Appliances/white goods	1/7/96	96	7.1	3.67
Anhui Expressway	Toll roads	1/11/96	113	22.2	1.77
China Eastern Airlines	Aviation	1/2/97	250	10.6	1.38
Shenzhen Expressway	Toll roads	1/3/97	185	20.8	2.20
Beijing Datang	Power generation	1/3/97	406	12.0	2.52
Beijing Northstar	Residential propert	1/5/97	191	13.5	2.40
Zhejiang Expressway	Toll roads	1/5/97	384	43.9	2.38
Total			**4,838**		

1. Placed 400mn new shares at HK$2.45 in April 1995, raising US$126.7mn

Sources: Company prospectuses

Table X.5: US N share listings as at May 1997

Company	Sector	Date listed	Funds raised (US$mn)	Listing P/E (weighted)
Brilliance China[1]	Automotive	1/5/88	80	18.0
Ek Chor Motorcycle*	Automotive	1/6/93	102	23.9
China Tire*	Automotive	1/7/93	83	24.3
Shanghai Petrochem	Petrochemicals	1/7/93	189	12.5
AES China*	Power generation	1/2/94	160	na
Huaneng International	Power generation	1/5/94	625	25.6
Shandong Huaneng	Power generation	1/7/94	333	18.4
Yuchai International	Automotive	1/12/94	75	9.7
Jilin Chemical	Petrochemicals	1/7/95	93	8.4
Guangshen Railway	Transport/railway	1/5/96	236	11.7
Total			**1,976**	

1. Listed before the idea for H and N shares was hatched (1992–92)

* These companies are technically not N shares, as they were not selected for overseas listing under the same process as other H and N shares

Sources: Bloomberg; company prospectuses

Bibliography, sources

All historical macro data on China used in this book come to us either directly or indirectly from China's State Statistical Bureau, the People's Bank of China, the International Monetary Fund, or the World Bank. We have also updated some series using the data released in the *China Statistical Yearbook, 1996.*

The veracity of China's economic statistics have been called into question a number of times. We have often faced issues of trying to unravel changes in the compilation of data from year to year. However, government data is clear enough to illustrate the big picture of China's economic development. To seek to adjust published data would invite its own difficulties.

Chapters 1, 2, 3

"Bank of China's Cultural Revolution", *Euromoney,* April 1996.

"Chain Mail Suits", *Far Eastern Economic Review,* March 7 1996.

The China Analyst, various editions, The Bank Credit Analyst Research Group, Montreal.

China at the Threshold of a Market Economy, Occasional Paper No. 107, International Monetary Fund, September 1993.

China Directory 1995/6, Radiopress, Inc, Tokyo.

China International Trust and Investment Corp., Moody's Investors Services, March 1995.

China Review, 1993, 1994, 1995, 1996, Chinese University Press, Hong Kong.

China Statistical Yearbook, 1996, China State Statistical Bureau.

Deng Xiaoping: Chronicle of an Empire, Ruan Ming, Westview Press, Boulder, 1992.

Effects of recent reforms on the credit quality of China's specialized banks, Moody's Investors Service, 1995.

Guangdong Statistical Yearbook, 1996.

Guangdong, Survey of a Province Undergoing Rapid Change, Y.M. Yeung, Chinese University Press, Hong Kong, 1994.

"PLA Inc", Tai Ming Cheung, *Institutional Investor,* July 1996.

Princes and Princesses of Red China, Ho Pin and Gao Xin, Mirror Books, Toronto, 1993.

"Social Capital and the Global Economy", Francis Fukuyama, *Foreign Affairs*, Volume 74 no. 5, 1995

Transforming China's Economy, S. Feuchtwang, Westview Press, Boulder, 1988.

Chapter 4

Almanac of China's Finance and Banking (various issues): English edition, Editor Board of Almanac of China's Finance and Banking, Beijing.

"*The Banker* top 1000", *The Banker*, July 1996.

"Bank-industry linkages: models for Eastern European economic restructuring", R.C. Smith, and I. Walter, In: D.E. Fiar, and R.J. Raymond (eds.): *The new Europe: evolving economic and financial systems in East and West*, Kluwer Academics, Dordrecht etc, 1993.

"Banking and finance in China", J.H. Zhang, and J.X. Zheng, KPMG, Hong Kong, 1994.

"Banking in China's economic reform", N. Lardy, Prepared statement to the Committee on Banking and Financial Services of the US House of Representatives (unpublished), Washington DC, March 20 1996.

China financial outlook, (various issues), The People's Bank of China, China Financial Publishing House, Beijing.

China's international banking and financial system, P.D. Reynolds, Praeger Publishers, New York, 1982.

China Securities Market Yearbook 1995, China Securities Regulatory Commission, Beijing.

China Statistical Yearbook (various issues), China Statistical Publishing House, Beijing.

Global Development Finance — Volume 2: Country Tables, World Bank, Washington DC, 1997.

"Process and prospects of commercialising state-owned specialised banks", Z. Jiang, Conference Paper from the China Banking and Finance Reform International Summit, China World Hotel, November 1995, Beijing.

"The role of international banks in the transformation of the Chinese financial system", C.A. Katz, Doctoral Dissertation, University of St Gall, St Gall, 1997.

"Survey of Asia's commercial banks", *Thomson BankWatch* (various issues), Thomson BankWatch, Hong Kong.
"Waiting game for China's foreign banks", D. Wilson, *Banker,* 136:726, 1986.

Chapter 5

CITIC Beijing annual report, 1995.
Red Chips Directory, Wardley James Capel (now HSBC James Capel), 1993.

Chapter 6

CITIC Pacific annual report, 1995.

Chapter 7

China Statistical Yearbook 1996.
Guangdong Enterprises (Holdings) annual reports for 1992, 1993, 1994 and 1995.
Guangdong Investment Limited annual reports for 1992, 1993, 1994 and 1995.
Guangdong Investment Limited, convertible bonds prospectus, September 1993.
Guangdong Statistical Yearbook 1996.
Guangnan (Holdings) Limited listing prospectus, November 1994.
IFR Securities Data.

Chapter 8

"The Third Front: Defense Industrialization in the Chinese Interior," Barry Naughton, *China Quarterly* 115, Autumn 1988.
The Yearbook of Iron and Steel Industry of China, 1994.

Other titles from Asia 2000

Non-fiction

Cantonese Culture — *Shirley Ingram & Rebecca Ng*
Egg Woman's Daughter — *Mary Chan*
Getting Along With the Chinese — *Fred Schneiter*
*The Rise and Decline of the Asian Century** — *Christopher Lingle*
*Walking to the Mountain** — *Wendy Teasdill*

Fiction

Cheung Chau Dog Fanciers' Society — *Alan B Pierce*
Chinese Opera — *Alex Kuo*
Daughters of Hui — *Xu Xi (Sussy Chakó)*
Getting to Lamma — *Jan Alexander*
Hong Kong Rose — *Xu Xi (Sussy Chakó)*
Riding a Tiger — *Robert Abel*
Temutma — *Rebecca Bradley & John Sloan*

Poetry

Woman to Woman and other poems — *Agnes Lam*
New Ends, Old Beginnings — *Louise Ho*

Photo Books

Beijing Spring — *Peter & David Turnley*
USSR: The Collapse of an Empire — *Liu Heung Shing*

**Distributed in the United States by*
University of Washington Press, PO Box 50096, Seattle, WA 98145
and in Canada by University of British Columbia Press
6344 Memorial Road, Vancouver, BC V6T 1Z2

All other titles, please contact Asia 2000 Ltd
1101 Seabird House, 22–28 Wyndham St, Central, Hong Kong
tel (852) 2530 1409; fax (852) 2526 1107
email sales@asia2000.com.hk; http://www.asia2000.com.hk/